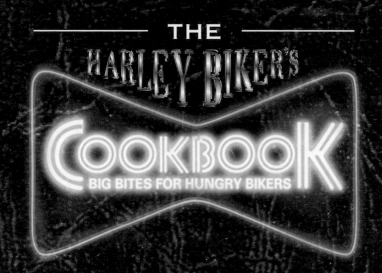

THE

HARLEY BIKER'S

COOKBOOK

BIG BITES FOR HUNGRY BIKERS

THE HARLEY BIKER'S

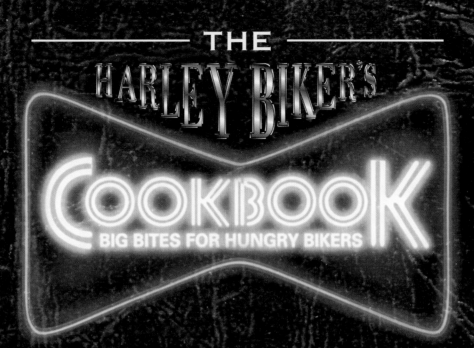

COOKBOOK
BIG BITES FOR HUNGRY BIKERS

OWEN ROSSAN

BIKER CONSULTANT
TOD RAFFERTY

CHARTWELL
BOOKS, INC.

Published by

CHARTWELL BOOKS, INC.
A Division of **BOOK SALES, INC.**
114 Northfield Avenue
Edison, New Jersey 08837

© Salamander Books Ltd. 2002

A member of **Chrysalis** Books plc

ISBN 0-7858-1531-7

Commissioning Editor: Will Steeds
Project Manager: Jane Donovan
Copy Editor: Alison Leach
Designer: Roger Hyde
Layout Production: Roger Lucas
Food Photography: Jon Stewart
Home Economist: Kathryn Hawkins
Location Photography: Garry Stuart
Color origination: Global Color Separation Ltd

Printed and bound by Kyodo Printing Company, Singapore Pte Ltd

Contents

15
Breakfast & Brunch

21
Appetizers

27
Meat Dishes

37
Poultry

43
Fish & Seafood

49
Vegetables & Salads

57
Sandwiches

63
Dressings, Sauces & Marinades

69
Desserts & Snacks

76-77
Index

FOREWORD

The abiding motto among Harley riders is *Ride to Live, Live to Ride*. Since eating is essential to life, and because preparing and sharing food with your friends is one of life's Good Things, the slogan of this book is *Ride to Eat, Eat to Ride*.

Anyone who has spent much time on a motorcycle knows the importance of food. Motorcycling is an actively physical undertaking; it requires acute hand-foot-eye coordination, keen perception, good judgment, and a certain measure of muscular strength. Eating well (and often) helps ensure the rider's ability to maintain those qualities on the open road. Likewise, the undernourished rider puts himself or herself at risk, and is more vulnerable to the effects of fatigue, cold weather, and diminished endurance.

Motorcycling and eating share the same fundamental requirement: balance. An unbalanced diet, like a destabilized motorcycle, can cause us to fall over. This is often painful. Doctors may necessarily be involved, and sometimes even lawyers. Life gets annoyingly messy, recuperation time drags on, the battery on your motorcycle goes dead, and the carburetor gets gummed up. And why? Just because you forgot Mom's simple admonition to eat a good breakfast.

Or—and this is just as important to the balance we seek—we forget the other essential component of the logical Eat to Ride program: exercise. Now there are some riders (you know who you are, and it's fairly obvious to the rest of us) who think this element is optional. But it ain't necessarily so. Just like the unburned fuel in a poorly tuned motorcycle, unburned food turns to sludge, clogs up the valves, and eventually brings the bodily machine to a sputtering halt. Or a sudden and abrupt seizure. Once again—pain, doctors, etc.

But please don't think that this is a "health food" cookbook, full of bland concoctions of curds and whey. Nay, this is Real Food for real bikers: delicious meals that will carry you through a long day's ride, and reward you with richly satisfying flavors at sundown.

So enjoy these foods, and share them with your saddlepals. In the words of Roland "Motoring" Jones, "Choose good friends, use good bread, eat well, ride long, and prosper." And always look both ways.

Tod Rafferty
Roadkill Raconteur

INTRODUCTION

Cooking is fun, but eating is even more fun. This has always been my motto. This is a cookbook for people who really like to eat. If you are the kind of person who thinks a few spoonfuls of cottage cheese with a squirt of catsup is lunch, a can of spaghetti or a tray of frozen something is dinner for two, then don't read any further. Firstly, that stuff isn't fit to eat. You can make much better and far more interesting food just as easily and more cheaply. And secondly, even if it tastes okay, the portions are ridiculous. Serving sizes in this book are for real eaters. When a recipe in this book says "Serves 2," it doesn't mean two dieters, but two hearty biker portions. In my family, you never left the table hungry — and you never will with these recipes!

Most cookbooks give instructions that sound as though there are no alternatives. The main thing to remember is that a recipe is just a suggestion—it is not the Ten Commandments or a speed limit. Every person has individual tastes and preferences. If you want to add more chili or less sour cream, or you don't like garlic, then just alter the recipe to your taste. You won't get arrested or get a ticket. And you don't have to follow the chapter headings. If you want the blue cheese soup for breakfast, the Mexican omelet for dinner or the stuffed mushrooms as a snack, then go right ahead. The only ones who have to like it are you and the people you cook for, not some author! Don't be shy, don't be timid, be creative. Cooking is supposed to be enjoyable and not hard work.

◆ Cooking Hints

With ordinary ingredients you can create a lot of extraordinary dishes or variations on old favorites. Use things like sour cream, balsamic vinegar, Worcestershire sauce, or soy sauce to enhance or change the flavor. Try using different spices; use maple syrup or honey instead of sugar; add a little mustard or coffee to intensify a flavor in a sauce or a whole dish. Rub a roast with garlic, cumin, paprika and sugar, as well as freshly ground salt and pepper just a few hours before roasting. Brush tomato halves with oil and shake on some salt, pepper and sugar. Roast in a very low oven for about five hours (yes, five hours!) until wrinkly, then eat warm or cold. Always taste as you go along: if it doesn't taste right, just keep fiddling around until you get it "right," i.e., the way *you* like it.

◆ Shortcuts

Many people grudge the time and preparation needed for cooking. But there are ways to make it faster and easier by "cheating" or taking shortcuts. The microwave is great for some speedy steaming. For perfectly cooked sweetcorn or asparagus, place them in a dish covered with plastic wrap and microwave for a few minutes. An artichoke takes just ten

minutes. Alternatively, in just a few minutes onions or bell peppers can be pre-softened before you sauté them. Or you can pre-cook chicken pieces for a few minutes before barbecuing. Microwave sauces for a few minutes before simmering or melt cheese, butter, or chocolate. It's not usually necessary to make your own mayonnaise or salsas when you can buy decent ones that you can jazz up with extra olive oil or sour cream, or some fresh cilantro and vinegar. And use a blender to mix sauces, eggs, or dressings.

A salad doesn't have to be the same old boring thing every time. Add some olives, anchovies and grated cheese to make it more interesting, topped with a vinaigrette dressing. For a great vinaigrette in minutes, just add some olive or salad oil to wine vinegar, salt, pepper, a little sugar and some mustard. Use about three parts oil to one part vinegar. Use a whisk to mix it together until it emulsifies. Make a whole lot of vinaigrette and keep it handy in a screw-topped jar in the refrigerator — it lasts for quite a long time.

When lemons are cheap and plentiful, buy lots of them. You can wash and cut them into thin slices, place on a sheet of waxed paper in a single layer and then freeze. Once frozen, place the slices in an airtight plastic container and keep in the freezer. Add a slice to cold drinks such as iced tea, lemonade or fizzy drinks. The lemon gives the drink a nice tang and helps to keep it cold or you can use limes or oranges in the same way for a different flavor.

Keep pasta, canned tomatoes and tomato sauce in your cupboard and store a hunk of parmesan cheese in your refrigerator. (Note: never use store-bought ready grated cheese; it tastes like soap and is far more expensive than grating your own for quick pasta dishes.) Add a can of chopped clams to a can of tomato sauce for an instant Spaghetti Vongole (Clam Sauce). Or sauté some chopped garlic, add a can of tomatoes, chopped anchovies and olives for another instant sauce.

When ice cream is too solid to dish out straight from the carton, pop it in the microwave for a few seconds, then serve. It also tastes so much better when it isn't rock hard! For a really great ice cream topping, microwave some peanut butter, mixed with a little milk, on low power until it is gooey to make a hot peanut fudge sauce. Or you could do the same with your favorite candy bar for a change of topping. The possibilities are endless.

A number of the recipes and ideas featured in this book come from a great old New Orleans cook, Louise Washington, and her friend Melanie Feldman. Others are just off-the-wall things that I played around with until I liked the way they tasted. That's the fun of cooking — getting ideas from friends and fooling around in a creative way. Be free, cook free!

Owen Rossan
Author

SHOTGUN WILLIE'S
SKI SHOP
RENTALS SALES
WELCOME, BIKER
OPEN
4 0 3

BREAKFAST
& BRUNCH

When Mom said breakfast was the most important meal of the day, she was right. Since some riders tend to skip lunch, or eat little more than a snack, breakfast assumes even greater significance. The genuine hot set-up is an adult portion of carbohydrates and proteins, accompanied by milk or fruit juice. Even if lunchtime finds you far out of town, you have energy in reserve to get on down the road.

ON THE MENU

Suzie's
Sour Cream Pancakes

Cheesy French Toast

El Paso Omelet

Cajun Fried Matzos

American Heritage
Biscuits

Kickstart Corn Bread

Jalapeño Horsepower Grits

Suzie's Sour Cream Pancakes

Delicious on their own, even better with your choice of berries.

<u>Serves 4</u>

<u>INGREDIENTS</u>

1½ cups all-purpose flour
1 tsp sugar
2½ tsp baking powder
¼ tsp baking soda
dash of salt
2 large eggs
7 fl oz milk
6 Tbsp melted butter
⅔ cup sour cream
1 cup of any berries, e.g. strawberries, blackberries, raspberries, blueberries
oil, for frying

1. Sift the flour and mix with the sugar, baking powder, baking soda, and salt.

2. In another bowl, beat in one egg at a time and then add the milk, melted butter, and sour cream. Add the flour mixture and mix well. Mix in the berries gently.

3. Heat and oil a griddle or heat a skillet with a thin covering of oil. Ladle out 3 tablespoons of batter for each pancake onto the griddle or skillet and fry till brown on one side (1 to 2 minutes). Turn and cook till brown on that side (1 to 2 minutes). Serve with syrup or jam and strong coffee.

Cheesy French Toast

The addition of cheese makes this slightly different from the usual French toast.

<u>Serves 2 to 3</u>

<u>INGREDIENTS</u>

6 slices bread (not fresh, but not stale)
3 large eggs
6 ounces grated cheese (Cheddar, Swiss, or any hard cheese you like)
½ tsp nutmeg
butter, for frying

1. It is important that the bread is not too soft or it won't hold the coating. If it is very soft, stick it in the oven for about 10 minutes on low heat to dry it out, not toast it.

2. Put the eggs, cheese, and nutmeg in a blender and beat till the cheese is blended and the mixture well mixed and frothy. Pour into a bowl and soak the bread in the mixture, at least 10 minutes on each side.

3. Heat a large skillet and add enough butter to cover the pan when melted. When the butter gets foamy, take the bread out of the egg mixture, let the excess batter drain off, and put in the skillet. Fry till brownish, then turn and fry the other side. Take out of the pan immediately. The toast should be slightly puffed up.

4. Serve with jam or syrup and crispy bacon.

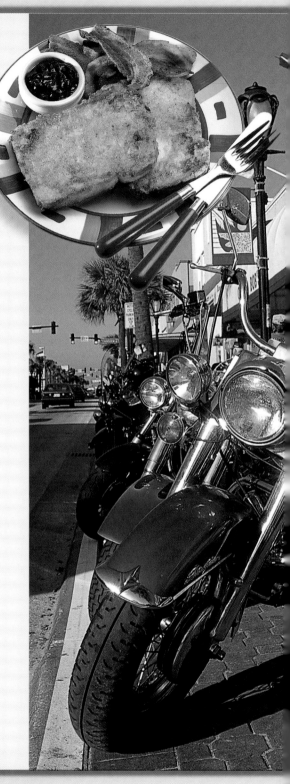

EL PASO OMELET

More substantial than the usual omelet, finishing it off under the broiler gives it a wonderful texture.

INGREDIENTS

oil, for frying
½ small onion, chopped
1 cup cooked potato (a cold baked potato is fine), diced
3 oz chorizo (spicy salami), chopped
3 green chilies, seeded and chopped
6 large eggs
1 Tbsp milk
⅛ tsp cayenne
¼ tsp salt
1 cup shredded Monterey Jack cheese (or other hard cheese)
sour cream
chopped cilantro
fried tortillas broken into quarters, to garnish
hot salsa

1. In a cast-iron skillet (this is important because it must be able to go under the broiler—if you don't have one, you can use a regular skillet and transfer to a heatproof casserole), pour in some oil and put over a low heat. Add the onion and fry gently for about 5 minutes or until somewhat soft.

2. Add the potato, chorizo, and green chilies. Continue to cook over a medium heat for about 5 minutes, stirring now and then to prevent the mixture sticking.

3. Beat the eggs, milk, cayenne, and salt till frothy. Turn up the heat under the pan until the oil is very hot (you may have to add some more oil here if the first amount has been absorbed, use your judgment). Give the ingredients in the pan a stir and pour in the frothy eggs, making sure the mixture surrounds, if not covers, all the other ingredients. As the eggs start to set, pull the edges back with a fork to allow any uncooked egg to hit the bottom of the pan.

4. When the eggs are almost set, remove the pan from the stove and sprinkle the grated cheese on top, covering the whole omelet. Put under the broiler on a low heat until the omelet is solid and the cheese is bubbly brown.

5. Remove to a heated platter, put a few spoons of sour cream on top, and sprinkle on the chopped cilantro. Garnish with fried tortillas along the sides. Cut into serving pieces and serve with the hot salsa on the side. Try this dish with hot chocolate, sprinkled with cinnamon, to drink.

CAJUN FRIED MATZOS

This is a spicy twist on an old Jewish favorite. You can spice it up or down as you like.

SERVES 2

INGREDIENTS

4 sheets matzos
4 eggs, beaten
¼ cup chopped chives or
green onions
½ cup milk
1 tsp sugar
Worcestershire sauce
Tabasco sauce
butter, for frying

1. Break up the matzos into pieces and put in a bowl. Pour enough boiling water into the bowl to cover the matzos. Cover the bowl with a plate and let sit for about 3 or 4 minutes.

2. Drain the water from the bowl. Add the beaten eggs and the chopped chives or green onions, together with the milk and sugar. Mix well. Add 3 or 4 dashes each of Worcestershire sauce and Tabasco.

3. Melt some butter in a pan (a nonstick one is best). When the butter starts to turn brown, add the matzo mixture, pressing it down into the pan to form a "pie." Cook over medium heat until the bottom is light brown. Flip over and brown the other side.

4. When ready, slide it out of the pan and cut into wedges. Sprinkle with more chopped onion or chives, to garnish. Serve with sour cream and strong black coffee.

KICKSTART CORN BREAD

This is quick and easy to prepare, making it ideal for breakfast.

INGREDIENTS

1 box (about 8½ ounces) of cornbread mix
(the kind that you just add water and
eggs)
3 Tbsp finely chopped jalapeño chilies
1 cup canned corn (drained)

1. Prepare the cornbread mix according to the directions on the box. Stir in the jalapeño chilies and the corn, and bake according to the directions, but add on 2 or 3 minutes to the baking time.

2. Remove from the oven and let cool for a few minutes. Cut into squares and serve with butter, strawberry jam or honey, and plenty of hot coffee.

AMERICAN HERITAGE BISCUITS

Quick and easy to make, just right for busy morning breakfasts.

MAKES ABOUT 12-15 BISCUITS

INGREDIENTS

2 cups all-purpose flour
2½ tsp baking powder
1 tsp salt
⅓ cup corn oil
1 cup milk

1. Sift the flour and put in a bowl with the baking powder and salt; mix together. Blend in the oil, making sure that it is entirely absorbed in the flour mixture. Pour the milk in slowly, while stirring.

2. When it is blended, use a large spoon to drop the batter onto a greased baking sheet. Bake in a 450°F oven until brown, about 15 minutes. Serve with butter, jam or honey, and scrambled eggs and bacon.

JALAPEÑO HORSEPOWER GRITS

Grits lend themselves to strong flavors, and these grits prove the point. The cheese, bacon, and chili make these a great start to the morning.

SERVES 4

INGREDIENTS

3 cups water
¾ cup easy cook (not instant) grits
½ cup grated hard cheese (Cheddar, Monterey Jack)
4 Tbsp jalapeño chilies
4 slices crispy bacon, finely crumbled
4 slices crispy bacon, cut in half
Tabasco sauce (optional)
sour cream (optional)

1. In a saucepan, boil the water, then slowly stir in the grits. Turn the heat to medium and give the grits a few stirs. When they start to thicken, stir in the grated cheese. As this melts, throw in the jalapeños (if you can take them in the morning) and the crumbled bacon, and cook for another minute or so until thick.

2. Pour into four soup bowls and garnish each with two pieces of the bacon on top and, if you like, a shake of Tabasco and a blob or two of sour cream. Great with scrambled eggs, toast and jam, and strong coffee.

Note If you don't use the jalapeños, at least the Tabasco should be used.

"I've got two favorite destinations when it's time for a long ride. One is a bed-and-breakfast inn up in the Sierra Mountains, where they make the world's best crêpes and fritters. And I'm not telling you the name of the place.

"The other one is the home of my old riding buddy Hank Simmons in New Mexico. He's one of the best refrigerator cooks in the country; meaning throwing together the leftovers in the refrigerator. But his specialty is catching and grilling rainbow trout. Fantastic."

Dallas McGrath, Colorado

19

APPETIZERS

◆

The trick with appetizers, as everyone knows, is knowing when to stop eating them. One solution is to make them only in limited quantities.

But good appetizers do just that: prompting the appetite for the main course and enhancing that preliminary glass of beer. They help us shift the mental gearbox from the chores of the day back into neutral, coasting for the warm relaxation of the dinner table. Just watch not to spill anything on the couch, and don't spoil your appetite.

ON THE MENU

Thunder Grunt
Stuffed Mushrooms

Norm's Nasty Nachos

Manny's Fried
Mozzarella Sticks

Billy's
Buffalo Wings

Claude's Blue
Cheese Soup

THUNDER GRUNT STUFFED MUSHROOMS

The high load of garlic gives these mushrooms their kick, but it does blend in with the rest of the stuffing. The secret here is to let the butter drip down into the mushrooms after it has "filtered" through the stuffing.

SERVES 2 TO 3

INGREDIENTS

10 mushroom caps (these should be as large as possible to hold the stuffing. If you can't find big ones, try and get flat ones)
3 strips bacon
¼ cup (½ stick) butter
2—3 cloves garlic, finely minced
½ cup fresh bread crumbs
1½ Tbsp Worcestershire sauce
¾ cup grated Parmesan cheese
5 Tbsp grated Parmesan, for topping

1. Remove the stems and clean and dry the mushrooms. Fry the bacon until crisp and crumble when cool. Keep the grease in the skillet.

2. Heat the bacon grease in the skillet and add the butter (you may need slightly more or less depending on the amount of bacon grease). Sauté the garlic slowly for about 5 minutes. Stir it around, then stir in the bread crumbs, and fry for another few minutes.

3. Add the Worcestershire sauce and the ¾ cup cheese and, finally, the bacon. Mix once again and cook for a few more minutes. When everything is well blended, remove from heat. The mixture should be very moist, but not wet. If there is too much liquid, add a little more bread crumbs and heat through.

4. Stuff the mixture into the mushrooms very tightly and top with a ½ Tbsp or so of grated Parmesan cheese. Put the stuffed mushrooms on a baking dish.

5. Place in a 350°F oven for about 20 minutes or until the cheese on top is brown. The main thing is to cook slowly enough to allow the butter to drip down into the mushrooms. Take the mushrooms out and put on paper towels to blot up any excess butter.

Serve with a glass of wine.

"Sometimes on a real long ride you'll start to fantasize about food. Images of delicious meals begin to materialize in your mind, and you start thinking about how good they would taste if it weren't the middle of the night and you weren't a couple hundred miles from the nearest all-night diner. So you have to get by on just these imaginary dishes, and after awhile it's almost as if you are experiencing the actual flavors as you ride along. Eventually the hunger goes away, replaced by the thought that you might be going crazy."

Gordon C. Childress, Indiana

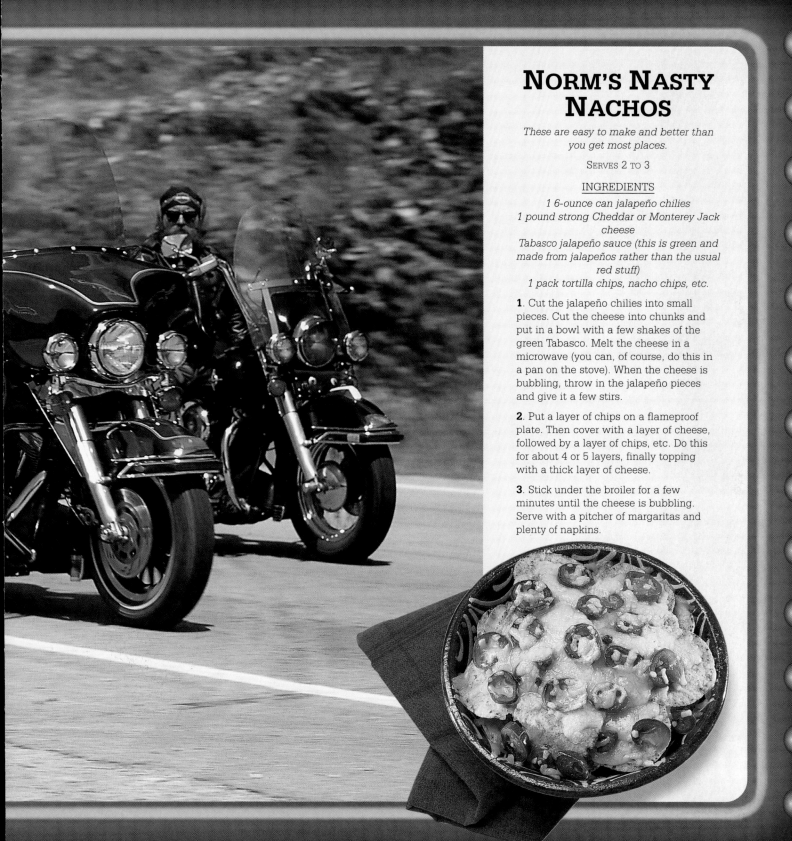

NORM'S NASTY NACHOS

These are easy to make and better than you get most places.

SERVES 2 TO 3

INGREDIENTS

1 6-ounce can jalapeño chilies
1 pound strong Cheddar or Monterey Jack cheese
Tabasco jalapeño sauce (this is green and made from jalapeños rather than the usual red stuff)
1 pack tortilla chips, nacho chips, etc.

1. Cut the jalapeño chilies into small pieces. Cut the cheese into chunks and put in a bowl with a few shakes of the green Tabasco. Melt the cheese in a microwave (you can, of course, do this in a pan on the stove). When the cheese is bubbling, throw in the jalapeño pieces and give it a few stirs.

2. Put a layer of chips on a flameproof plate. Then cover with a layer of cheese, followed by a layer of chips, etc. Do this for about 4 or 5 layers, finally topping with a thick layer of cheese.

3. Stick under the broiler for a few minutes until the cheese is bubbling. Serve with a pitcher of margaritas and plenty of napkins.

MANNY'S FRIED MOZZARELLA STICKS

Perhaps not the best diet food, but with some lively dips, they sure are good.

SERVES 3 TO 4

INGREDIENTS

1 pound mozzarella cheese
2 eggs
½ cup dry bread crumbs
1 tsp cajun spice
oil for frying

1. Cut the cheese into "fingers" about ⅜ by ⅜ by 3 inches. Beat the eggs. Combine the bread crumbs with the spice and put the "fingers" in the egg, and then into the bread crumbs.

2. Heat some oil in a heavy skillet to about ¼-inch depth. When hot, but not smoking, fry the battered cheese until golden brown, turning when necessary. This takes about 1 minute.

3. Remove with a slotted spoon and serve immediately. These can be eaten on their own, but they go well with dips such as Carolina BBQ Marinade, page 67, the sauce in Billy's Blue Cheese Buffalo Wings, opposite, sour cream and chives, or mayonnaise spiked with salsa, or just plain salsa. Make sure there is plenty of beer to wash it all down.

CLAUDE'S BLUE CHEESE SOUP

This is a soup with a difference. The blue cheese gives it a deep, richly satisfying flavor. You can use Gorgonzola, Stilton, or Roquefort instead if you like any of those better. And it is really simple to make.

Serves 4

INGREDIENTS

¼ cup (½ stick) butter
3 onions, sliced
2 Tbsp all-purpose flour
4 cups chicken stock or canned chicken consommé
6 ounces blue cheese, crumbled
⅔ cup heavy cream
dash of nutmeg
salt and pepper
croutons and chopped parsley, to garnish

1. In a saucepan over low heat, melt the butter. Add the onions and cook slowly until they are soft.

2. Add the flour and stir over low heat until all the flour is absorbed and slightly cooked. Gradually stir in the chicken stock, making sure there are no floury lumps left.

3. Bring to a boil, take off the heat, and stir in the crumbled blue cheese, the cream, nutmeg, salt and pepper to taste. Pour into individual serving bowls and garnish with croutons and chopped parsley. Serve with warm French bread and butter, and a glass of wine.

BILLY'S
BUFFALO WINGS

Is there anyone in the world who doesn't know the wings story? If not, you can still enjoy this dynamite (literally!) recipe. If you can't stand the heat, don't get out of the kitchen, cut down on the hot spices.

SERVES ABOUT 4 AS AN APPETIZER

INGREDIENTS

2 pounds chicken wings
salt
oil, for frying

SAUCE

2 cups canned tomato sauce
2 tsp minced garlic
1 Tbsp horseradish sauce
1 tsp crushed red pepper/crushed chilies
1 tsp cayenne pepper
1 tsp garlic powder
1 tsp Tabasco

1. First make the sauce. Combine all the ingredients in a saucepan and heat until almost boiling. Turn down the heat to low and prepare the wings.

2. Cut the tips off the chicken wings and discard. Then cut the wings at the joint so you have two pieces. Salt the wings and let stand for a while.

3. Heat the oil in a heavy skillet and fry the wings until brown and cooked through. Drain the wings and put in a bowl to cool.

4. Pour over enough of the heated sauce to cover the wings. Mix well so all the wings are coated with the sauce. Tip out onto a warm platter and serve immediately with the chilled blue cheese dressing (right), stalks of celery, and a fire extinguisher. A cold beer would also be nice.

BLUE CHEESE DRESSING

INGREDIENTS

6 ounces blue cheese
1/2 cup mayonnaise
1/2 cup sour cream
1 tsp Worcestershire sauce
1 Tbsp lemon juice
1 Tbsp dry sherry
1 tsp minced garlic
dash of pepper

1. Put all the ingredients in a blender and mix for a few seconds. If not fully mixed, hit it for another few seconds. Don't overbeat the mixture

2. If it gets too thin, thicken up with a little mayo beaten in by hand. Chill before serving with the wings.

"Sometimes the setting is just as important as the food. Breakfast always tastes better around a campfire than it does in a restaurant, and lunch is usually more satisfying in your own kitchen than in a fast food dispensary.

"Of course there's no denying the convenience factor of eating out, including the bonus of having no dishes to clean. But it's a bit like having someone else work on your motorcycle; just not as satisfying as doing it yourself."

Jack Randall, New Hampshire

MEAT DISHES ◆

othing beats a well-prepared chunk of beef. The methods of cooking meat vary widely throughout America, the number magnified by mixed ethnic traditions. But the most important consideration is matching the cut of beef with the style of preparation, as in barbecued short ribs.

Of course good beef is available everywhere in America and with regional variations comes the long roster of ways to cut and cook. You should not spend any time in a major metropolis without sampling the best steak in town. Be sure to stop in Kansas City.

ON THE MENU

Lone Star BBQ Spareribs

Carmelita's Fajita Skirt Steak with Guacamole

Fried Ham Steak & Red Eye Gravy

Torque Master Meatloaf

Benjie's Beijing Spareribs

Lenny's Lemon BBQ Short Ribs

Fat Sam's Stuffed Pork Chops

Louise Washington's Best Chili (& Even Better Chili & Beans)

Bad Boy Beef Tacos

Nicole's Nostalgia Lasagne

Marty's Brewhouse Brisket

Ricki Sue's Beef Barbecue

Lone Star BBQ Spareribs

Spareribs cooked slowly with a great sauce—is there anything better?

SERVES 2

INGREDIENTS

2 slabs pork spareribs
salt

SAUCE

1 minced onion
3 cloves garlic, minced
1 Tbsp sage
3 Tbsp Worcestershire sauce
1 tsp Tabasco sauce
1 cup catsup
¼ cup lemon juice
¼ cup vinegar
1 tsp dry mustard
1 tsp celery salt
¼ cup brown sugar
1 tsp cayenne
1 tsp chili powder

1. Cut all fat off the ribs and make a 1-inch cut between each rib at both ends. Sprinkle lightly with salt.

2. Heat gently all the sauce ingredients for about 30 minutes, stirring occasionally. Do not let boil.

3. Put the ribs on a rack, rib side up and cook in a 400°F oven for 15 minutes. Turn down the oven to 325°F. Turn the ribs over and coat with sauce, and cook for 30 minutes, basting after about 15 minutes. Then turn the ribs over, baste, and cook for another 30 minutes or until done.

4. Take the ribs out of the oven, and serve along with any extra sauce. Serve with French fries, coleslaw, warm French bread, and lots of cold beer.

Note The ribs can be cooked slowly over charcoal and take about an hour or so to cook.

Carmelita's Fajita Skirt Steak with Guacamole

This is a great way to make any steak, but is best made with skirt steak. A bit less messy eating than fajitas, but the same set of flavors.

INGREDIENTS

1 large skirt steak (about 1½ pounds)

MARINADE

½ cup salad oil
1½ Tbsp ground cumin
3 cloves garlic, finely chopped
½ tsp salt
½ tsp sugar
1½ Tbsp lime juice
2 Tbsp chopped fresh cilantro or freeze-dried, if fresh is unavailable
few shakes of Tabasco

1. Mix the marinade ingredients together and let stand for 15 minutes.

2. Put the steak into the marinade, turning it a few times to cover all of it with the marinade. Marinate overnight if you can, but at least for 4 or 5 hours. Give it a couple of turns while it is marinating.

3. Drain off the marinade. Broil the steak under a very hot flame or over charcoal, turning and basting with marinade until cooked to your liking.

4. Serve with guacamole (recipe opposite), soft fried onions, a medium salsa, and warm flour tortillas, accompanied by a cold Mexican beer.

GUACAMOLE

INGREDIENTS

1 ripe avocado
2 Tbsp finely chopped onion
1 Tbsp lime juice
few shakes of Tabasco
salt (this needs lots of salt)
1 jalapeño chili, finely chopped

1. If the avocado is not ripe, put it in the microwave on low for about 5 minutes. Split the avocado, remove the pit, and scoop out the flesh into a bowl.

2. Mash it slightly with a fork, then add the other ingredients, and mash some more, mixing everything in. There are two guacamole schools: the rough and the smooth. If you are the latter, keep mashing, but don't make it into a purée as it loses all its character.

"Tell you what—barbecue is about the best thing that God ever came up with. If heaven is any kind of place at all, they'll have barbecue every day. Some folks fancy beef, but tell you what—you get a fine pork butt out of the smokehouse, barbecue it with some good sauce, and that meat just falls off the bone. That's heaven right there."

Emmet Johnson, South Carolina

FRIED HAM STEAK & RED EYE GRAVY

Known as Red Eye Gravy in the South, the fried salty flavor of the ham is perfectly set off by the sweet coffee gravy.
Pass the biscuits.

SERVES 2

INGREDIENTS
2 ham steaks, about ¼ inch thick (don't remove the fat)
3 Tbsp dark brown sugar
1 tsp sugar
⅓ cup strong black coffee

1. Remove the rind from the ham steaks and score the fat. Brush the ham steaks with the brown sugar and let sit for about 10 minutes.

2. Then place in a heavy skillet over a low heat. When the bottom is brown (about 6 to 8 minutes), turn over and sprinkle a little more brown sugar on the top side of the ham (make sure the sugar doesn't burn). When the second side is brown, check to see that the steaks are fully cooked. If not, lower the heat and cook until done. Remove to a warm platter.

3. Mix the teaspoon of sugar into the coffee and pour into the pan. Turn up the heat and scrape the stuck-on pieces off the bottom of the pan. When the coffee is almost boiling, taste the gravy and, if too bitter, add a little more sugar. Pour over the ham steaks and serve them with eggs, biscuits, and plenty of hot coffee.

BENJIE'S BEIJING SPARERIBS

Does anyone go to a Chinese restaurant and not order these? Make these at home, put them in a white container, and pretend you ordered in.

SERVES 2

INGREDIENTS

1 slab (about 2½ pounds) pork spareribs (or lamb if you want)

MARINADE
½ cup tightly packed dark brown sugar
½ cup real Chinese soy sauce
¼ cup catsup
1 Tbsp dry sherry
1 tsp minced garlic
1 tsp minced fresh ginger

1. Trim off all the fat from the ribs and make about ½-inch cut between each rib on both the top and bottom. This is to allow the marinade to penetrate and to make the ribs more tender, when cooked.

2. Pour the marinade over the ribs, making sure that the whole slab is covered with the sauce (not submerged). Let stand for about 4 hours, less if you are in a hurry.

3. Put the ribs on a rack, bone side up, and roast in a 350°F oven for about 35 minutes. Turn the ribs over and baste with the marinade a few times while cooking. If still not fully cooked, turn the oven up a bit and cook until done. They should be a glistening reddish-brown color, but still moist.

4. Cut into individual ribs, stack on a platter, and serve along with the Sweet-Funky Dunking Sauce, page 67 and Mi Hung's Mustard Sauce, page 66. Serve with fried rice, a stir-fried green vegetable, and a Chinese beer.

TORQUE MASTER MEATLOAF

This meatloaf is crunchy, punchy and you can still eat it cold in sandwiches.

SERVES 4

INGREDIENTS
1 pound ground beef
1 pound ground pork
oil, for frying
2 onions, sliced
2 green bell peppers, chopped
4 stalks celery, chopped
2 x 8-ounce cans water chestnuts, sliced
4 cloves garlic, chopped
2 cups sliced mushrooms
2 tsp ground pepper
2 tsp thyme
4 tsp paprika
2 tsp dry mustard
4 tsp celery salt
4 tsp sugar
3 tsp Tabasco sauce
5 Tbsp soy sauce
4 Tbsp Worcestershire sauce
4 tsp lemon juice

1. Mix the beef and pork together in a large bowl.

2. In a skillet, pour in some oil and cook the onions slowly. Just before they turn brown, add the green bell pepper, celery, water chestnuts and the garlic. As they get soft, turn up the heat and add the mushrooms and cook for a few minutes.

3. Turn down the heat and add the pepper, thyme, paprika, dry mustard, and celery salt. Cook for a few more minutes and add the sugar, Tabasco, soy sauce, Worcestershire sauce, and lemon juice. Stir in and heat for a minute.

4. Let sit for about 15 minutes and then mix into the meat. Place in a casserole. Cook in a 350°F oven for about 1—1½ hours until done.

5. Strain off any grease and cut into serving pieces and serve with mashed potatoes and taco sauce or catsup.

LENNY'S LEMON BBQ SHORT RIBS

Beef short ribs are an under-rated cut of meat, mainly due to their fattiness and toughness. The lemon in the sauce solves this problem and makes these a nice change from the usual pork spareribs.

SERVES 4

INGREDIENTS
4 pounds beef short ribs

MARINADE
½ cup lemon juice
3 cloves garlic, minced
¾ cup brown sugar
1½ tsp chili powder
½ cup canned tomato sauce
1 tsp salt

1. Mix the marinade ingredients well and pour over the short ribs. Turn the ribs so they are all coated with the marinade. If there isn't enough marinade to coat the ribs, make a "half order" of the marinade and add to the ribs. Marinate for about 3 hours, more if you have time.

2. Place the short ribs in a covered casserole, pour over the marinade, and cover. Put in a 350°F oven for about 45 minutes. Remove the ribs from the casserole with a slotted spoon.

3. Then place the ribs on a broiling rack or over a charcoal grill and broil slowly for about 20 minutes until they are brown and crispy on all sides.

4. While the ribs are broiling, take the sauce from the casserole and skim off the grease. Pour it into a bowl and freeze for about 10 minutes. The grease will have solidified and can easily be removed.

5. Boil the remaining sauce up for a few minutes to reduce it, and serve alongside the ribs. Garlic bread and a green salad are the perfect accompaniments.

Note You can broil the ribs, skipping the baking, but they must be broiled very slowly to allow proper cooking. Baste with the sauce while broiling.

FAT SAM'S STUFFED PORK CHOPS

*These pork chops have an Italian bias and deglazing
the pan with balsamic vinegar gives it a
wonderful taste.*

SERVES 4

INGREDIENTS

*2 cloves garlic, finely minced
4 double thick loin chops (have the
butcher cut a deep pocket in each chop
for stuffing)
1 tsp sage
1 tsp oregano
1 tsp rosemary
½ cup fresh bread crumbs
1 or 2 Tbsp olive oil
2 Tbsp chopped green olives
salt and pepper
about 2 Tbsp olive oil
⅓ cup balsamic vinegar
⅓ cup water*

1. Using your hands, rub the garlic all
around the inside of the pockets in the
pork chops.

2. Mix the sage, oregano, and rosemary
well with the bread crumbs. Add some
olive oil to make it slightly moist. Don't
make it too moist or it will fall out of the
pockets when cooking. Stuff some of the
mixture into each of the chops.

3. Then make a pocket in the mixture and
put a quarter of the olives in each bread
crumb pocket.

Add a little of the bread crumb mixture to
seal the pocket. Then close and seal the
chops using two or three toothpicks on
each. Salt and pepper the chops.

4. Heat 2 Tbsp olive oil in a heavy
casserole and brown the chops on both
sides. If there is no oil left in the casserole,
add another spoon or two of oil to prevent
sticking. Then cover the casserole and
place in a 350°F oven for about 45 minutes
or until done. Test by piercing with a
skewer—the juices should run clear.

5. Remove and place on a warm platter.
Put the casserole on the stove over
medium heat, and pour in the balsamic
vinegar and water, scraping the bits off
the bottom. Heat for a few minutes till all
the bits are mixed in. Taste the sauce for
seasonings and if the vinegar taste is too
strong, add a little
more water. This is
not meant to be a
gravy, but rather a
bit of sauce to
complement the
meat. Pour over the
chops. Serve with a
green salad and a
glass of red wine.

BAD BOY BEEF TACOS

*The different garnishes allow each taco to
be custom-built. You are the designer—let
your imagination run wild.*

SERVES 2

INGREDIENTS

*oil, for frying
1 onion, chopped
3 cloves garlic, finely chopped
1 pound ground beef
1 tsp cayenne
1 tsp oregano
1 tsp cumin
1 tsp chili powder
salt and pepper
8 corn tortillas or taco shells*

GARNISHES

*shredded lettuce
grated Monterey Jack cheese
chopped jalapeño chilies
chopped cilantro
bottled taco sauce
guacamole
sour cream*

1. In a large skillet, pour in some oil and
gently cook the onion for about 5 minutes.
Add the garlic and meat to the onion and
fry for a few minutes. Add the spices and
herbs with salt and pepper to taste, and
mix well, continuing to fry until the meat
is fully cooked. Drain and keep warm.

2. If you are using tortillas, wrap them in
tin foil and warm in a low oven for a few
minutes until soft.

3. Spoon some of the meat mixture into a
tortilla and garnish with any or all of the
above. Put the "drier" items on first,
followed by the "wetter" ones. Fold the
tortilla over and eat. It is important not to
overfill the tortillas or it all falls apart.

4. If you are using taco shells, follow the
same procedure (except for the folding bit)
and caution. The most interesting way to
eat these is to vary the toppings so that
each taco is a new taste sensation.

5. Serve with refried beans and a beer.

Louise Washington's Best Chili
(& Even Better Chili & Beans)

This dish is a combination of two parts— the meat and the beans. The first part (the meat) can be eaten on its own, but is even better with the beans, page 50.

INGREDIENTS

3 Tbsp oil
2 large onions, finely chopped
1 large green bell pepper, seeded and sliced
1-2 cloves garlic, minced
2 pounds lean ground beef
1 Tbsp all-purpose flour
2 stalks celery, finely chopped
1 16-ounce can whole tomatoes
1 6-ounce can tomato sauce
1½ cups water
¼ cup chili powder (or to taste, i.e. hotter)
1 tsp cumin seed, ground
1 Tbsp sugar
salt and pepper

1. In a large, heavy skillet, heat the oil and brown slowly the onion, green bell pepper, and garlic. Mix the beef and flour together. Add to the skillet and cook until very brown.

2. Add the remaining ingredients with salt and pepper to taste. Cover the skillet and cook for 30 minutes over medium heat, stirring.

3. Top with sliced jalapeño chilies and shredded cheese (if you like), and serve with fried tortillas and cold beer.

4. For even better chili, add the above to Good Old Boys' Barbecued Beans, page 50. Cover the skillet and simmer for 1½ hours. Stir every so often and add more water, if necessary. Serve as above.

> "I reckon my favorite feast of the year is our annual pig roast on the Fourth of July. All the bikers show up the day before, and we get the pit dug and start the fire. The next day we have field events on our bikes, eat the pork, and shoot off fireworks. We just have a helluva good time."
>
> Prewitt Cadwallader, Tennessee

BREAKFAST PIZZA
SALADS INDIAN
POLISH DOGS TACOS
NACHOS

33

RICKI SUE'S BEEF BARBECUE

This is a bit extravagant, but worth it. The secret is the Pickapeppa Sauce made in Jamaica, West Indies. You can find it in specialty food marts.

SERVES ABOUT 4 OR 5

INGREDIENTS

1 beef tenderloin filet (about 3 pounds—this is the cut that filet mignon steaks are cut from)
2 Tbsp garlic, finely mashed
salt and pepper
5 or 6 Tbsp Pickapeppa Sauce
5 Tbsp sugar
melted butter
chopped parsley, to garnish

SAUCE

3 Tbsp dry sherry
3 Tbsp melted butter
3 Tbsp Pickapeppa Sauce

1. Trim the meat of all fat and wipe dry. Using your hand, rub the roast all over with the garlic, salt and pepper, and the Pickapeppa Sauce. Let sit for about 15 minutes. Then rub the sugar over the meat.

2. Set the broiler on high and broil the meat for about 20 to 30 minutes, depending on how well done you like it. (25 minutes should give you a medium rare fillet). The sugar will burn and seal in the juices. While broiling, baste with melted butter, and as you turn it over.

3. When cooked, put the meat on a heated platter and "rest" for 5 minutes.

4. In the meantime, take a small saucepan and add the dry sherry, melted butter, and Pickapeppa Sauce. Let your tastebuds be a guide, but start out with the equal amounts first. Heat gently and then add the juices from the platter.

5. Cut the beef into thick slices and pour the heated sauce over it. Garnish with some chopped parsley and serve with crusty French bread, sautéed potatoes, a green salad, and a hearty red wine.

NICOLE'S NOSTALGIA LASAGNE

This version comes from a friend's mother and is the best I have found.

SERVES 6

INGREDIENTS

1 8-ounce can tomato paste
3 cups canned tomatoes
1 tsp salt
1 tsp freshly shredded basil
1 tsp sugar
2 bay leaves
2 cups water
2 cloves garlic, finely chopped
2 Tbsp olive oil
1 pound Italian sausage, chopped
1 tsp dry oregano
1-pound package lasagne noodles
1 cup grated Parmesan cheese

CHEESE MIXTURE

2½ pounds ricotta cheese
1 large egg
3 Tbsp sugar
½ tsp salt

1. Combine the tomato paste, the canned tomatoes and their juice, salt, basil, sugar, bay leaves and the water and simmer for about 2½ hours.

2. Gently brown the garlic in the olive oil and add the sausage meat and oregano. Stir in the tomato sauce and continue to simmer until cooked through.

3. Boil the pasta in plenty of boiling water according to the package directions. Drain.

4. For the cheese mixture, combine the ricotta, egg, sugar, and salt well.

5. Sprinkle the base of a large casserole with one-third of the Parmesan cheese. Add a layer of half the tomato sauce, a layer of half the pasta, then a layer of half the cheese mixture. Repeat these layers. Sprinkle the remaining Parmesan cheese on top. Put in a 375°F oven for at least 20-25 minutes until piping hot. Serve with a green salad and a hearty red wine.

"Good barbecue depends on several important factors: the type of fuel, the amount of heat from the coals, and the distance between the meat and the coals.

"Charcoal briquets are the standard fuel for most family barbecues, but really authentic cooking requires a hardwood fire using oak, hickory, or mesquite. It takes longer for the wood to burn down to ash, but the aromatic flavoring is worth it. Be sure to keep a water spray bottle on hand to douse flare-ups from dripping fat."

Mike Wisnewski, Kentucky

MARTY'S BREWHOUSE BRISKET

Although brisket can be dry and stringy, this is tender and the beer gives it a delicious flavor.

<small>SERVES ABOUT 6 DEPENDING ON THE SIZE OF THE BRISKET</small>

INGREDIENTS

2 cloves garlic, mashed
1 large beef brisket, trimmed of all fat, at least 3-4 pounds
1 large onion, sliced
5 stalks celery, sliced
½ green or red bell pepper, sliced
1 medium-size bottle of chili sauce
salt and pepper
1 12-ounce can full-bodied beer
6 carrots, peeled and cut into 1-inch slices
4 large potatoes, peeled and cut into 8 equal pieces
½ pound mushrooms (whole)

1. Rub the mashed garlic over the brisket, coating it.

2. In a heavy casserole, place the brisket and surround it with the onion, celery, and sliced bell pepper. Pour the entire bottle of chili sauce and a few tablespoons of water over the meat. Add salt and pepper to taste.

3. Place in a 450°F oven till the meat is brown (about 30 minutes). Cover the casserole and reduce heat to 300°F. Simmer in oven for about 3 hours until almost tender.

4. Add the beer, carrots, potatoes, and mushrooms. Cover the casserole again and cook for another hour. Check the seasoning.

5. Slice the meat, place on a serving platter, and surround it with the carrots, potatoes, and mushrooms. Pour the remaining liquid in the casserole over the meat. Serve with French bread to mop up the juices, a green salad, and a cold beer.

POULTRY

C hicken and turkey have always figured strongly on traditional home-cooking menus. Whether you like your poultry grilled, braised, baked, fried or barbecued, you're never too far from either a restaurant or market with all the fixings. Included here are several tasty recipes from areas where the well-prepared bird is regarded with almost religious reverence. There are spots in Kentucky where it's extremely risky to come between a man and his fried chicken. Of course, if you're polite, he's likely to share it with you. Feel free to lick your fingers!

ON THE MENU

Sara Liz's
Garlic & Honey Chicken

Sweet Jean's
BBQ Chicken Wings

Blue Bayou
Fried Chicken

Down Home
Deep-Fried Turkey

SARA LIZ'S GARLIC & HONEY CHICKEN

These are really easy to make, but delicious just the same.

SERVES 2 TO 3

INGREDIENTS

salt
10 chicken pieces; thighs and drumsticks work best but any cut pieces will do
6 cloves garlic, minced
6 Tbsp honey
chopped chives, to garnish

1. Salt the chicken pieces and rub them all over with the garlic. Let sit for about 15 minutes.

2. Put the chicken pieces in a roasting pan, making sure that the garlic is still on the pieces. Make sure the pan is big enough so that you don't have to stack up the pieces. Roast in a 400°F oven for about 20 minutes.

3. Take the pan out and drain off any liquid (not the garlic) that has accumulated. Pour the honey over the chicken making sure that each piece is well covered. If you need more honey for this, then use it.

4. Roast for 20 more minutes or until the chicken pieces are crisp and shiny brown. Put on a warm platter and sprinkle with chopped chives. Serve with mashed potatoes and buttered green peas.

"We rode down to New Orleans once, and made it a point to sample all the barbecue we could along the way. Now that was a memorable trip.

"We met some real interesting folks on the ride, and ate some of the finest barbecued pork and beef you can imagine. Some people were glad to share their recipes with strangers, others just smiled and said it was a family secret. There's quite a variety in barbecue sauces, and it's fun to try as many as possible."

Buster Campbell, Illinois

Sweet Jean's BBQ Chicken Wings

These are less fiery than Billy's Buffalo Wings (see page 25) and are more suited to being served as a main course.

SERVES 2

INGREDIENTS

12 chicken wings, with the tips removed

SAUCE

1 tsp dry mustard
1 tsp water
1 x 8-ounce can tomato sauce
4 Tbsp maple syrup
1 tsp Worcestershire sauce
2 Tbsp brown sugar
1 Tbsp lemon juice

1. First make the sauce. Put the dry mustard in a bowl and add the water to dissolve the mustard. Add the other sauce ingredients. Mix together and heat in a saucepan for about 5 minutes. Let stand for 15 minutes.

2. Add the chicken wings and toss until they are all coated with the sauce. Let stand for an hour or so.

3. Take the wings out of the marinade and put them on a broiling rack, bone-side up, and broil under a low heat. When brown, turn them over, baste with the sauce, and broil until crispy.

4. Boil up the remaining marinade and serve on the side. Serve with garlic bread and coleslaw.

Blue Bayou Fried Chicken

This fried chicken has a more interesting crust than usual due to the added spices.

SERVES 3 TO 4

INGREDIENTS

1 cup all-purpose flour
½ tsp celery salt
½ tsp pepper
½ tsp garlic powder
½ tsp paprika
¼ tsp cayenne
1 frying chicken, about 3 pounds, disjointed
oil, for frying
1 cup milk

1. Mix the flour and spices together in a paper bag. Dry the chicken pieces thoroughly and put a few pieces at a time into the paper bag; shake well to coat. Remove the floured pieces and repeat until all the pieces have been coated.

2. In a heavy skillet with a lid, put enough oil to make a depth of 1½ inches and heat until hot, but not smoking. Put in enough of the chicken so that each piece is touching the bottom of the skillet. Cover and cook until the bottom of each piece is brown (about 8 minutes).

3. Turn the pieces and cook, uncovered, until that side is brown. Turn down the heat and fry for about 5 to 10 more minutes until the juices run clear when pricked with a fork. Remove with a slotted spoon and put on a warm platter. Fry the remaining pieces of chicken in the same manner.

4. Pour off most of the oil from the skillet and put it back on the stove. Pour in the milk and stir, scraping the bottom to get all the good crunchy bits. Throw in a few drops of hot sauce if you like. If it looks too floury, add a bit more milk. When it almost boils, pour into a gravy boat and serve alongside the chicken, not on top. Serve with mashed potatoes, biscuits, and honey, and iced tea to drink.

"We really like a good bird. Chicken or turkey, mostly, duck or pheasant now and then. Maybe some Cornish game hens.

"It's surprising how many good ways there are to cook poultry, and you can season it with just about anything you want. A lot of the best chicken recipes are from the south, but there are plenty of Asian and Mexican dishes that are outstanding. Not to mention the variety of chicken sandwiches."

Irv Weissberg, New Jersey

DOWN HOME DEEP-FRIED TURKEY

This is a mind-blowing way of making boring turkey interesting. The dark and white meat taste entirely different. Although you need a lot of oil, you can drain it, refrigerate it and reuse it, if you like the results, which I am sure you will.

SERVES ABOUT 6 TO 8

INGREDIENTS

*1 small turkey
salt
3 Tbsp mashed garlic
shrimp and crab boil-in-a-bag spice
2 to 3 Tbsp chopped red chili peppers
about 8 cups oil, for frying*

1. Dry the turkey thoroughly and rub with salt. Put the mashed garlic, bag of shrimp and crab spice and chopped chili peppers in the oil. You must have a cooking pot that is large enough to take the whole turkey. Heat the oil slowly in the pot until it is boiling hot. Carefully and slowly lower the turkey into the oil, breast-side down. If there is not enough oil to completely cover the turkey, then add enough to cover it.

2. Keep the heat high enough so that the oil continues to boil. (The skin will start to bronze.) After about an hour, test for doneness by moving a leg up and down. If it moves easily and can be pulled away from the rest of the bird, it is ready.

3. Slowly take the turkey out of the oil and drain thoroughly. Place on a heated platter and let rest for about 10 minutes before carving. Serve with candied yams and cranberry sauce.

Note McCormick and Zatarain's both make the above spice, which is a "bouquet garni" of mustard seed, coriander, red pepper, bay leaves, dill, allspice, and cloves packed in a cheesecloth bag.

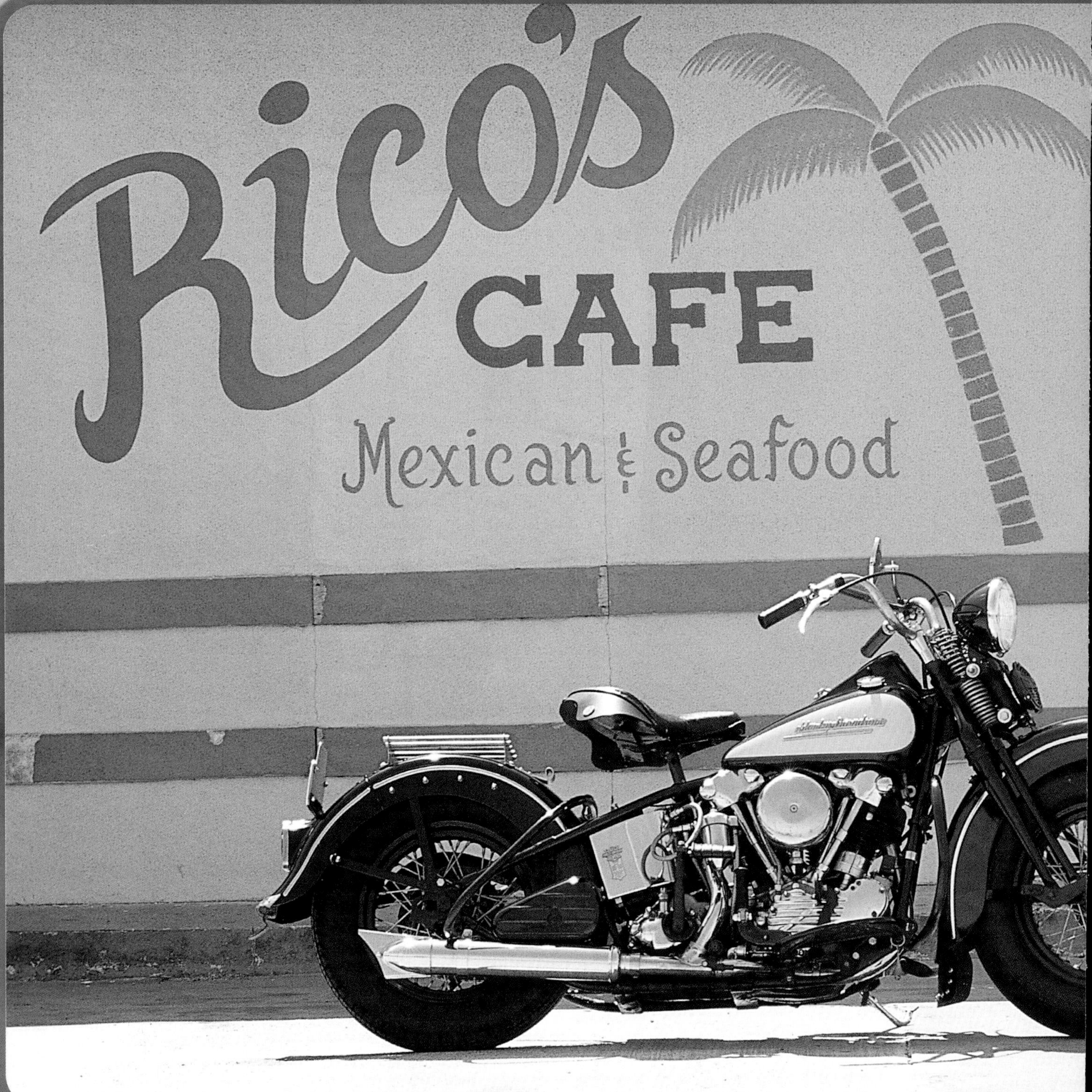
Rico's
CAFE
Mexican & Seafood

FISH & SEAFOOD

◆

S eafood is well established as a good source of protein, and should certainly contribute to a diet of balanced nutrition. Since there are plenty of fish in the sea, enough to feed both us and the bigger fish, it follows that fish must be healthy to survive and proliferate in such numbers. So it takes only a short leap of reasoning to conclude that some of that healthfulness passes to us at the dinner table, and that we absorb some of the power and mystery of the ocean. Don't we?

ON THE MENU

Crab & Shrimp
Au Gratin

Sal Calamari's
Seafood Salad

Bubba's Original
BBQ Shrimp

Bike Club Soda Fried Fish

CRAB & SHRIMP AU GRATIN

This can be made with either all shrimp or all crab, if preferred, but using both makes it a more interesting dish.

SERVES 2

INGREDIENTS

¼ cup (½ stick) butter
1 or 2 tsp all-purpose flour
1 cup heavy cream
2 green onions, chopped
1 cup grated sharp Cheddar cheese
½ tsp sugar
1 tsp Worcestershire sauce
salt and white pepper
few dashes of Tabasco
½ pound crabmeat
½ pound peeled shrimp
2 Tbsp bread crumbs
chopped parsley

1. Melt the butter in a heavy iron skillet. Add the flour and stir into the butter over low heat. When blended, add the cream slowly and then add all the other ingredients except the seafood, bread crumbs and parsley. Blend in over *low* heat for 2 or 3 minutes.

2. Fold in the seafood. Transfer the mixture to a baking dish and sprinkle with the bread crumbs. Bake in a 350ºF oven for about 15 minutes until bubbly.

3. Sprinkle with chopped parsley and serve on toast points with a salad and a chilled white wine.

SAL CALAMARI'S SEAFOOD SALAD

Quick to make, a tangy mustard mayo makes this a perfect summer dish. The seafood can be lobster, crab or shrimp, or a combo of all three.

SERVES 2 TO 3

INGREDIENTS

1 pound seafood
slice of lemon
3 stalks celery, chopped
¾ cup Mustard Mayo (page 66)
few shakes of paprika
a handful of chopped
parsley, to garnish

1. Put the seafood in a bowl and give it a squirt of lemon. Add the celery and mustard mayo and mix well. Refrigerate for about an hour.

2. When ready to serve, sprinkle on the paprika and garnish with the chopped parsley. Serve with French fries and a cold dark beer.

"The most crucial thing in cooking, once you get the proper mix of ingredients and seasoning, is knowing when the food is done. If it's undercooked or overcooked, it's just not worth the candle.

"This is true of everything: meat, seafood, poultry, and vegetables. The problem is that people's tastes run from rare to well-done, or so they think. Most of the time it's just eating habits from childhood, when we ate it the way Mom cooked it. Truth is, the food itself has an optimum point of preparation; the trick is achieving it."

Bernard Grossman, Vermont

BUBBA'S ORIGINAL BBQ SHRIMP

This is a great dish, from an old New Orleans "secret recipe." It is much better cooked with raw shrimp with the heads on, which gives it its special flavor.

SERVES 2 TO 3

INGREDIENTS

²/₃ cup oil
¹/₃ cup butter
1 Tbsp crab boil seasoning
1 lemon—the juice plus the peel
dash of sugar
dash of salt
1 pound raw shrimp with the heads on
lemon wedges and parsley, to garnish

1. Simmer the oil, butter, crab boil, lemon juice and peel, and the dash of sugar and salt together in a pan.

2. Put the raw shrimp in a broiling pan and pour the oil mixture over the shrimp. The oil mixture should come up to the edge of the top of the shrimp, but not cover them. If there is not enough liquid to do this, make some more, keeping the proportions the same.

3. Broil for about 5 minutes under a medium heat or until the shrimp are pink. Then turn the shrimp over and broil on the other side.

4. When cooked, put the shrimp in individual soup bowls and ladle some of the sauce over them. Garnish with lemon wedges and parsley. Serve with crusty French bread to mop up the sauce, a green salad, and a cold beer.

Note Crab boil is a liquid seasoning used for seafood cooking, for which there is no real substitute, but if you can't get it, then you can use any seafood seasoning.

"We usually don't carry much food on long rides. If we're camping with a group, we just buy food in the nearest town and cook it at the campground. My husband takes his fishing gear, so sometimes we're frying fresh trout right after it's been caught. Some of our best dinners have been outdoors."

Jackie Ashbaugh, Minnesota

BIKE CLUB SODA FRIED FISH

The soda water is what makes this different from ordinary fried fish. Any firm white fish will do, but cod is especially good this way. Frozen fish is OK, but be sure it is well defrosted and dry.

SERVES 2

INGREDIENTS

3–4 fillets of fish, about 1 pound
3 Tbsp all-purpose flour, to coat
oil for frying
6 Tbsp cornstarch
about ²/₃ cup soda water (not mineral water)
½ tsp cayenne
½ tsp paprika
½ tsp salt
½ tsp onion powder
½ tsp garlic powder
¼ tsp oregano
¼ tsp thyme
chopped parsley, to garnish
½ cup orange marmalade
½ cup prepared horseradish

1. Wash the fish fillets and pat dry with paper towels. Coat the fillets thoroughly with the flour. Set aside. In a heavy skillet, start the oil heating.

2. Prepare the batter: In a *glass* bowl, make a mixture of the cornstarch and soda water that will flow freely off a spoon. Mix the spices, salt, and herbs together and add to the batter.

3. Dip the floured fillets in the batter and fry until light brown. When done, put on a heated platter. Pour off the oil from the skillet and scrape the crispy brown bits from the pan. Sprinkle the bits on top of the fish along with some chopped parsley.

4. Serve with a dipping sauce of the orange marmalade mixed with the prepared horseradish, and a green salad.

VEGETABLES
& SALADS

V eggies offer such broad combinations of flavors and textures that you have to pity the poor souls who seem unable to eat anything green.

Of course fruit, vegetables, and grains can compose a healthful menu on their own, but are far more fun with meat and poultry. Fresh vegetables offer a host of complementary flavors to the main course, and leftovers can easily be recycled for another meal.

So eat your vegetables!

~ ON THE MENU ~

Good Old Boys' Barbecued Beans

Mark's Macaroni & Cheese

Dave's Deluxe Potato Salad

Dial 911 Mashed Potatoes

Robyn's Spicy Fried Okra

Mean Green Bean Casserole

Spuds Rodriguez' Hot Potato

Good Old Boys' Barbecued Beans

These are the real southern red beans—good enough to eat on their own, but even better when combined with Louise's chili recipe (page 33) or served over boiled rice as a main course dish.

Serves 4

INGREDIENTS

1 pound dry red kidney beans (soaked overnight in water)—canned can be used but they are not as good
3 Tbsp bacon fat
1 large yellow onion, finely chopped
1 green bell pepper, seeded and finely chopped
2 large cloves garlic, minced
1 ham hock with some meat on it
1 bay leaf
dash of thyme
dash of Tabasco
dash of salt
4½ cups water
2 Tbsp chopped parsley

1. Drain the beans. In a heavy iron pot, melt the bacon fat and sauté the onion, green bell pepper, and garlic for 3—4 minutes until softened. Add the beans and all the remaining ingredients except the parsley.

2. Bring to a boil and boil rapidly for 10 minutes, then lower the heat. Cover the pot and cook slowly over low heat for 4 hours, stirring from time to time.

3. When cooked, add the parsley and stir, replacing the cover. Let the beans cool slightly.

"You can do a lot with beans. Back in the midwest we always had beans just steamed as a side dish; limas and green beans, or kidney beans in chili, lentils in soup.

"Here in the far out west, beans get fixed in all kinds of ways, and they are often combined with vegetables and grains in some interesting ways. This is a good way to get a substantial dose of protein without eating lots of meat. And you get lots of good fiber and vitamins in the bargain. Also, black beans and rice is known to cure melancholia."

Morgan Stolwicz, California

MARK'S MACARONI & CHEESE

Choose pasta with a larger diameter so the sauce can get inside.

SERVES 4 AS A SIDE DISH

INGREDIENTS

½ pound uncooked rigatoni, penne or
other tubular pasta
½ stick butter
3 Tbsp all-purpose flour
1 cup milk
1 tsp garlic powder
1 Tbsp Dijon mustard
½ cup grated sharp Cheddar
½ cup grated Swiss cheese, such as
Emmenthal or Gruyère

1. Cook the pasta until "al dente."

2. In a saucepan over low heat, melt the butter. Stir in the flour until the butter is absorbed. Add the milk slowly while continuing to stir. Stir in the garlic powder and the mustard. Then add the two cheeses and stir until blended into a smooth thick sauce.

3. Put the cooked pasta into a buttered casserole and mix in the sauce, ensuring that it entirely covers the pasta. Bake in a 400°F oven for about 15 minutes until brown and heated through. Put under the broiler for a minute or so to make the top crispier if you like. Serve as a side dish to grilled pork sausages or with strips of cured ham. This can be zoomed up a bit with a dash of Tabasco added to the sauce, or sprinkle crisp, crumbled bacon over the top as a garnish.

DAVE'S DELUXE POTATO SALAD

Potato salad with a zippy garlic-flavored mayo goes with just about any meat or chicken.

SERVES 4

INGREDIENTS

1 cup mayonnaise
3 cloves garlic, very finely minced
½ tsp lemon juice
4 cups cooked potatoes, skinned and diced
½ cup thinly sliced celery
½ cup finely chopped green onions
salt and pepper

1. Put the mayo, garlic, and lemon juice into a blender and blend for 30 seconds. Let sit for about 15 minutes.

2. Pour the garlic mayo over the potatoes, celery, and green onions. Toss and add salt and pepper to taste. Serve with fried chicken, spareribs or broiled pork sausages.

Note If you like it spicy, add 1 teaspoon of finely chopped fresh green chilies to the mayo.

DIAL 911 MASHED POTATOES

You may need to dial 911 after eating these potatoes, but it is worth it. They are so rich they only need some simple broiled meat or fish as an accompaniment.

SERVES 4

INGREDIENTS
2 pounds potatoes
½ cup heavy cream
6 Tbsp melted butter
cayenne pepper
salt and black pepper
freshly chopped parsley

1. Peel the potatoes and boil until they are soft.

2. While they are cooking, warm the cream slightly. When the potatoes are cooked, drain and put them back in the pan over a low heat. Mash the potatoes using a potato masher or a grater. *Do not use a blender or food processor unless you want glue.*

3. Slowly add the melted butter and beat into the potatoes. When well blended, add the warm cream in the same way. Keep stirring until smooth and creamy. Sprinkle in a few shakes of cayenne pepper. Add salt and pepper to taste. Sprinkle with freshly chopped parsley.

Note This dish takes a lot of salt.

"One thing you have to remember about potatoes is that they can explode in the oven. I didn't know you were supposed to poke 'em with a fork before baking. They can be a real chore to clean up, let me tell you.

"But it's just a real marvel the number of ways you can fix up potatoes, like with vegetables, meat, and cheese on top. My old man likes 'em with chili and onions; I put broccoli, cheese and bacon bits on mine. Real easy to do and makes a meal in itself."

Tamara Shannon, Texas

ROBYN'S SPICY FRIED OKRA

Crunchy like popcorn, spicy, and with a slight taste of fried oysters, this is really great.

SERVES 2

INGREDIENTS
1 pound fresh okra, washed
salt
2 Tbsp Tony Chachere's Cajun Spice, Louisiana Seasoning, Old Bay Seasoning, or Lawry's Season Salt
2 medium eggs, beaten
about ½ cup oil for frying

1. Trim off the ends of the okra and cut into ½-inch thick slices. Put in a colander and salt. Let drain for 10 minutes.

2. Mix enough of the spice mixture into the beaten eggs to get a thick, but still runny, mixture. Mix in the okra and let sit for 15 minutes.

3. Pour enough oil into a heavy skillet to cover the bottom to a depth of about ¼ inch. While the oil is heating, give the okra mixture one more stir and then lift it out with a slotted spoon to drain off the excess egg mixture.

4. When the oil is hot, place half the okra in the skillet. Separate the pieces so they don't stick together and fry for about 2 or 3 minutes until brown. Remove with a slotted spoon and put on paper towels to drain. Keep warm. Repeat with the remaining okra. Check for salt and serve immediately with a seafood salad or other mayonnaise-based dish. Or just eat as a snack like popcorn.

Note The above directions are for young, tender okra. If you have older, tougher ones, boil or microwave (medium) for a few minutes before draining and tossing in the egg-spice mixture.

MEAN GREEN BEAN CASSEROLE

An old favorite of my mother's, made the real way it goes with just about any meat, fish, or fowl.

SERVES 6

INGREDIENTS

2 x 10-ounce packages frozen green beans
1 x 8-ounce can French fried onions

VEGETABLE MIX

¼ cup (½ stick) butter
½ cup chopped onions
1 x 8-ounce can mushrooms, drained and sliced
1 x 5½-ounce can water chestnuts, drained and sliced

SAUCE

¼ cup (½ stick) butter
¼ cup all-purpose flour
1 tsp salt
½ tsp pepper
1¼ cups milk
2 cups grated sharp Cheddar cheese
2 tsp soy sauce
¼ tsp Tabasco

1. For the vegetable mix, melt the butter in a skillet and sauté the onions, mushrooms, and water chestnuts for 5 minutes. Set aside.

2. For the sauce, melt the butter in a saucepan. Stir in the flour, salt and pepper, and cook slowly for 3 minutes. Do not let the mixture brown. Remove the pan from the heat and add the milk slowly, stirring to combine. Return the pan to the heat and cook slowly, stirring until thickened. Then add the cheese, reserving ¼ cup, stirring constantly. When the cheese melts, stir in the soy sauce and Tabasco. Set aside.

3. In a buttered baking dish, spread half the vegetable mixture, then half the green beans, and then half the cheese sauce. Repeat with the remaining ingredients in the same order. Sprinkle the reserved cheese on top.

4. Place in a 350°F oven for 15 minutes. Sprinkle the French fried onions on the top and bake for 10 more minutes. Serve piping hot.

"I've been all over this country on a motorcycle, and I've eaten some of the worst food and lots of the best food. After a while you know which places to stop and which to pass up.

"I could probably put together a pretty good book myself, listing all the best places in the country to eat. Maybe combine it with the best motorcycle roads, places to camp, sights to see and stuff like that. I wonder if anyone would publish a book like that?"

Earl Davidson, Wyoming

SPUDS RODRIGUEZ' HOT POTATO

This takes the boring old baked potato and sour cream to a new level. Try it with anything that "normal" baked potatoes go with. It is also a great snack.

SERVES 2

INGREDIENTS

1 medium jalapeño pepper, finely sliced
½ cup thick sour cream
2 baked potatoes (microwaved is fine)
¼ cup thick salsa or taco sauce
4 Tbsp grated strong Cheddar cheese
2 Tbsp chopped cilantro

1. Mix the sliced jalapeño pepper into the sour cream.

2. Cut open the potatoes horizontally and run a fork over the insides to create a rough surface. Make a little well in each half by spooning out some potato. Spoon a tablespoon of the salsa or taco sauce into each well. Put 2 tablespoons of the sour cream on each half, then a tablespoon of the grated cheese, and finally ½ tablespoon of the chopped cilantro. Serve immediately.

SANDWICHES

◆

Hail to the sandwich! No other food offers the marriage of nutrition, quick preparation, portability, and mouth-watering flavors of a good sandwich. Long-distance riders count on a satisfying sandwich as a restorative intermission to the rhythm of the road. The "fast food" version will do in a pinch, but a Real Sandwich serves both body and soul. So in gas stations throughout America, the question most often asked by bikers is, "Who makes the best sandwich in town?"

ON THE MENU

The Don's Sausage & Pepper Sandwich

Spread It On Hamburgers

Da Bears' Hot Dogs

Pit Stop Gyros

Rich Man's Po'Boy

Mario's Meatball Sub

MARIO'S MEATBALL SUB

Call it a sub, hero, or grinder, this is still a great sandwich.

SERVES 2 TO 3

INGREDIENTS

½ pound ground pork
½ pound ground beef
1 egg, beaten
2 cloves garlic, finely minced
2 ounces grated Parmesan cheese
salt and pepper
olive oil
1 x 8-ounce can tomato sauce
1 tsp oregano
green and black pitted olives, sliced
1 loaf Italian bread, split lengthwise
4 ounces Provolone cheese, sliced
hot Italian peppers, chopped

1. Mix the pork and beef with the beaten egg, garlic, Parmesan cheese, and salt and pepper. When well mixed, form into meatballs and fry in a little olive oil over a medium heat. Turn occasionally. When brown, remove with a slotted spoon and keep warm.

2. While the meatballs are cooking, put the tomato sauce in a pan with the oregano and the olives and heat slightly.

3. Split and brush the inside of the Italian bread with olive oil and warm slightly in a medium temperature oven.

4. Put the meatballs in the warmed bread and top with the tomato and olive sauce, and then the Provolone cheese. Drizzle with a little olive oil. Stick under the broiler for a minute or two to melt the cheese. Top with chopped hot Italian peppers and cut loaf into two or three pieces. Serve with lots of hearty red wine.

"One of my favorite sandwiches is the Reuben, which I hear got its name from a guy named Edelman in Jersey. He was eating one and somebody asked him what it was. But he thought they said 'how are you doing?' 'Real good,' he said. But with his mouth full, it sounded like he said 'Reuben.' Interesting, huh?"

Benjamin D. Watson, Pennsylvania

SPREAD IT ON HAMBURGERS

Different from a regular hamburger, they are cooked with the bun which gives a much more juicy, intense flavor. Topped with a slice of onion, it is a marvelous contrast of soft and crunchy, hot and cold.

SERVES 2 TO 3

INGREDIENTS

1 pound lean ground beef
½ cup catsup
2 tsp Worcestershire sauce
1 tsp garlic salt
1 tsp celery salt
4 large hamburger buns
1 onion, sliced thinly

1. Put the ground beef in a bowl and mix in the seasonings. Knead the mixture until it reaches a paste-like consistency. Let stand for about 15 minutes.

2. Meanwhile, split the buns lengthwise and toast. Spread the beef mixture evenly over the eight half buns. Be sure to cover every part of the bun. This is important so that the bun doesn't burn.

3. Place under a medium broiler and cook until done (even if you usually like your meat rare, it is best to cook until brown). When done, top with a thin slice of raw onion. Serve with a few slices of dill pickle and potato chips.

DA BEARS' HOT DOGS

Irresistible, the perfect lunch or snack, they must be made with the real McCoy. Is one ever enough?

MAKES ONE DA BEARS' HOT DOG

INGREDIENTS

1 Chicago hot dog
1 hot dog bun with poppy seeds
1 small onion, chopped
mustard
sweet pickle relish
slice of dill pickle
1 hot pepper
celery salt

1. This must be made with a real Chicago hot dog, not those funny little tasteless things sold in vacuum packs at the supermarket. The real thing is all beef with no filler, highly spiced with loads of garlic, and stuffed into a natural casing to hold in the juice. The 4-ounce monsters are the best size. Place in boiling water, turn down the heat and simmer for about 5 minutes. Be sure the skin doesn't split.

2. Meanwhile, steam the bun (this can be done in a microwave on low).

3. When both are ready, split the bun along one side and put the hot dog in, followed by the chopped onion, mustard, relish, the slice of dill pickle, and the hot pepper. A shake or two of celery salt and you are on your way to heaven. Serve with French fries and a Coke. You can eliminate any of the "trimmings," but do not use catsup as this is a crime against nature in Chicago.

RICH MAN'S PO' BOY

With the price of oysters, this is not for poor boys, but the crunch of fried oysters is delicious.

SERVES ONE GREEDY PERSON

INGREDIENTS

9 fresh oysters—more if you can afford it
½ tsp cayenne
½ tsp white pepper
½ tsp salt
oil for frying
1 cup milk
1 cup all-purpose flour
1 French bread, cut lengthwise
½ cup mayonnaise
Tabasco
shredded lettuce
sweet pickles, to garnish

1. Wash and dry the oysters. Mix the seasonings and add to the flour. In a heavy skillet, add oil to a depth that will just cover the oysters, and heat.

2. Dip the oysters in the milk and then the seasoned flour. Fry until they are golden brown.

3. While the oysters are frying, lightly toast the bread and spread with mayonnaise mixed with a dash of Tabasco.

4. When the oysters are ready, put on one piece of the bread and top with the chopped lettuce and the other piece of bread. If the bread is too long for the number of oysters, just chop off one end so that the oysters cover the entire length of the bread. Garnish with a few slices of sweet pickles and serve with a cold beer.

"There's no good reason to go hungry just because you're out in the backcounty on a motorcycle. There are all kinds of prepared foods you can carry along, like beef jerky or other snacks in your jacket. A small insulated cooler is easy enough to carry, especially the soft kind, and it will keep sandwiches and drinks cold. You can even wrap meat and potatoes in aluminum foil and reheat them on the exhaust pipe. And always carry water if you're riding in hot climates; dehydration is no fun."

Carl Ellison, Arizona

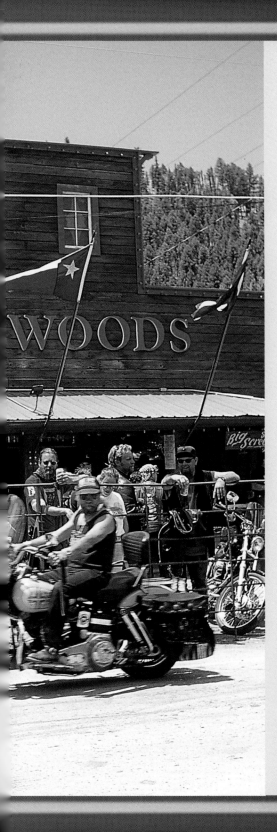

THE DON'S SAUSAGE & PEPPER SANDWICH

Either the sausage that comes in a continuous spiral or individual sausages are OK. Cut the spiral type into 6-inch lengths.

SERVES 1 TO 2

INGREDIENTS

1 green bell pepper, seeded and sliced
1 onion, sliced
2 cloves garlic, finely chopped
oil for frying
1 pound hot or mild Italian frying sausage
glass of red wine
1 loaf Italian bread
grated Parmesan cheese

1 . Put the green bell pepper and onion in the microwave for 5 minutes on medium. Drain off any liquid.

2. Fry the bell pepper, onion, and garlic slowly in a little oil in a heavy skillet. When the onion and pepper are soft and lightly brown, remove with a slotted spoon and keep warm.

3. Prick the skins of the sausages with a fork, and fry slowly until brown. When done, take the sausages out, and make the "sauce."

4. Turn up the heat and pour in the wine, scraping the bottom of the skillet to get off the crusty bits. When the wine boils, turn off the heat and stir.

5. Cut the bread into 6-inch lengths and slice lengthwise. Put one or two sausages in the bread. Spoon on some of the onion and pepper, pour over some of the "sauce," and then sprinkle with some grated Parmesan. Serve with a glass or two of red wine.

PIT STOP GYROS

While not the real thing, a quick, tasty imitation can be made with leftovers. Though lamb is more authentic, you can use what you have in the refrigerator.

INGREDIENTS

leftover roast lamb, pork, beef, or even chicken or turkey
small can (about 8 ounces) of tomato sauce
Tabasco
pocket bread (pitta)
salt
chopped onion
shredded lettuce or cabbage
hot peppers

1. Cut the meat into thin slices. If there is a bone, just hack out the bits you can get at. Warm in the microwave or oven.

2. Warm the tomato sauce in a pot or in the microwave and add a few drops of Tabasco. Warm a pocket bread in a medium microwave or oven until it blows up like a balloon.

3. Cut off a thin strip from the side of the pocket bread and open it. Toss in some meat, a few shakes of salt, then a spoon of sauce, some onion and lettuce or cabbage, some more sauce, and a few hot peppers. Make sure you don't overfill the pocket bread or else it will all fall apart in your hands. It goes well with a glass of red wine or beer.

"We get a lot of motorcycle racers who stop here to eat, with the track right down the road. They seem to be a pretty good bunch, and they surely can put away the food.

"Some of the boys must do real well. They've got big vans with names of large companies on the side. You would think some restaurant chain or food company would be a good sponsor for a motorcycle racer. They travel all over the country, and of course the kids look up to them. And most of them are such polite young men."

Ailene Graham, Florida

DRESSINGS
SAUCES & MARINADES

The importance of dressings and sauces often gets overlooked in the rush to put food on the table. We tend to settle for bottled preparations or excessive doses of salt, pepper, and butter.

But excellent sauces, marinades, and dressings are simple mixtures, easily and quickly prepared. And they give new dimensions of flavorful variety to foods that may have grown boring in their unrelieved sameness. The process also adds a measure of creativity to cooking, and lets you experiment with all sorts of flavors.

Just follow your nose.

ON THE MENU

Frenchy LeBec's Steak Sauce

Nutty Parmesan Dressing

Rudy's Russian Dressing

Guido's Creamy Garlic Dressing

Dutch's Mustard Mayo Dressing

Sweet-Funky Dunking Sauce

Mi Hung's Mustard Sauce

Carolina BBQ Marinade for Meat & Chicken

FRENCHY LeBEC'S STEAK SAUCE

A strongly flavored sauce that takes a minute to make, and goes perfectly with broiled steak or veal chops.

MAKES ENOUGH FOR ONE VERY LARGE STEAK

INGREDIENTS
2 ounces blue cheese
1½ tsp Worcestershire sauce
2 Tbsp butter

1. Put the blue cheese (at room temperature) into a bowl and mash it, while adding the Worcestershire sauce and blending together.

2. Melt the butter over low heat in a small saucepan (nonstick is best). Just as the butter melts, add the cheese mixture and mix into the melted butter. Stir until almost bubbling and pour immediately over a broiled steak or veal chop accompanied by a full-bodied red wine.

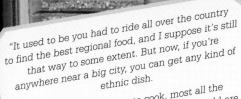

NUTTY PARMESAN DRESSING

An intense sauce that goes well with greens, hot or cold. Make sure to use real ungrated cheese, rather than the horrible, mass-produced, pre-ground stuff.

MAKES ENOUGH FOR 1 POUND OF COOKED ASPARAGUS OR BEANS

INGREDIENTS
*½ cup shelled walnuts
2 ounces Parmesan cheese or pecorino romano
½ cup olive oil*

1. Put the walnuts and cheese into a food processor and grind slightly. Slowly add some of the oil, making sure that it is absorbed into the walnut mixture. Give it a whirl or two and then add the remaining oil. The dressing should be the consistency of apple sauce.

2. Spoon over freshly steamed asparagus or green beans, or serve with steamed artichokes. To use as a salad dressing, add some additional oil to a few spoons of the mixture and toss with romaine or other strongly flavored green lettuce.

Note This dressing keeps in the refrigerator for a long time, but be sure to serve at room temperature.

RUDY'S RUSSIAN DRESSING

The chopped black olives and sour cream make this dressing a bit different from the usual version. Use on a salad of crisp greens with ham and Swiss cheese, a BLT, or a club sandwich.

MAKES ABOUT 2 CUPS

INGREDIENTS
*1 cup mayonnaise
½ cup chili sauce
¼ cup sweet pickle relish
½ cup sour cream
1 Tbsp horseradish
salt to taste
chopped black olives*

1. Mix all the ingredients except the olives for a few seconds in a blender. This gives it a nice consistency.

2. Add the olives and mix the dressing by hand. Serve chilled.

GUIDO'S CREAMY GARLIC DRESSING

A creamy rich dressing to serve with salad greens or a tomato and black olive salad.

MAKES ABOUT 2 CUPS

INGREDIENTS

1 cup sour cream
½ cup mayonnaise
¼ cup whole milk
2-3 tsp finely minced garlic or garlic purée
½ tsp anchovy paste
1 tsp tomato paste
salt and pepper
sugar (optional)

1. Put the sour cream and mayo into a blender. Whizz for a few seconds. Add the milk and whizz again. Add the garlic, anchovy paste, and tomato paste and whizz again.

2. Add salt and pepper to taste and a tiny bit of sugar if the garlic is bitter. Chill before serving.

> "Motorcyclists are generally good eaters. Not that all of them eat the best foods, but they tend to enjoy adult portions. They are not, as a rule, part of the diet brigade so widely promoted in the media. Any diet that is temporary is a sham.
>
> "Even overweight riders are usually in better health than most of the Nutrition Nazis. The single greatest problem most motorcyclists have, especially when that is their only recreation, is that they don't walk enough. The healthiest eaters are the regular walkers."
>
> Dr Steven Downing, Massachusetts

DUTCH'S MUSTARD MAYO DRESSING

The perfect dressing for seafood salad or as a dip for crunchy vegetables. It is also good on ham and cheese sandwiches.

MAKES 1 CUP

INGREDIENTS

1 cup mayonnaise (commercial or homemade)
2 tsp Dijon mustard
1 tsp lemon juice
½ tsp salt
1 tsp sugar

1. Put the mayo in a bowl and give it a few stirs. Using a fork, blend in the mustard, lemon juice, salt, and sugar. Since mustards differ in their strength, taste the mixture. It should have a smooth, not too pronounced "mustardy" taste. If necessary, add more mayo or mustard to obtain the desired taste.

2. Chill and serve over seafood salad.

MI HUNG'S MUSTARD SAUCE

Warning! This sauce is extremely powerful and is best served alongside Sweet-Funky Dunking Sauce (page opposite) for a real sweet and sour flavor.

MAKES ½ CUP

INGREDIENTS

4 Tbsp dry mustard
4 Tbsp water

1. Put the dry mustard into a bowl. Stir in the water slowly, mixing until it is smooth.

2. Serve in a white bowl and use for dunking spareribs, egg rolls, or roast pork.

Note This sauce is even better if you use some leftover white wine or stale beer instead of the water.

SWEET-FUNKY DUNKING SAUCE

Forget all those horrible bottled "plum" or sweet sauces—this is the best ever sauce for roast pork, chicken, and spareribs, or even egg rolls.

MAKES 2 CUPS

INGREDIENTS

½ cup dark brown sugar, tightly packed
10 whole black peppercorns —ground pepper is no good
½ cup plain old white vinegar—no fancy stuff here
1 cup apricot preserves or jam—not jelly
1 Tbsp cornstarch
2 Tbsp cold water

1. Put the brown sugar, peppercorns, and vinegar into a pan and heat gently, stirring now and then until the sugar has dissolved. Then stir in the apricot preserves slowly and cook gently for about 5 minutes or until the preserves melt.

2. While the mixture is heating, combine the cornstarch and water in a bowl, stirring until smooth. Then stir into the pan mixture and cook for a few minutes until the cornstarch is dissolved. Let cool and refrigerate.

3. Serve side by side with Mi Hung's Mustard Sauce (page left). If you have Chinese takeout, throw away those little plastic packs of junk and use this instead.

Note This sauce keeps for several months in the refrigerator stored in a jar with a screw-top cover.

CAROLINA BBQ MARINADE FOR MEAT & CHICKEN

This is an all-purpose marinade to put on meats or chicken before grilling.

MAKES ABOUT 1½ CUPS

INGREDIENTS

2 Tbsp ground cumin
4 cloves garlic, minced
2 Tbsp chili powder
2 tsp dry mustard
2 bay leaves
¼ tsp cinnamon
¼ cup sugar
1½ tsp celery salt
2 tsp paprika
2 tsp sage
6 Tbsp lemon juice
3 Tbsp Worcestershire sauce
1 tsp Tabasco
2 Tbsp cider vinegar
1 cup oil

1. Stir all the dry ingredients together in a bowl. Add the lemon juice, Worcestershire sauce, Tabasco, and cider vinegar. Stir and let sit for a few minutes.

2. Add the oil and mix well. Let sit for about an hour to allow the flavors to merge.

3. Coat meat or chicken with the mixture and marinate overnight in the refrigerator. The marinade also tenderizes, so you can use tougher (and cheaper) cuts than usual.

Note This marinade keeps for a long time in the refrigerator.

DESSERTS
& SNACKS

D esserts fall into two broad categories: those that are quick and easy to prepare and those that are not. Each has its place in the colorful spectrum of delicious sweets.

We know that fruits provide the healthiest desserts, and that they should be eaten regularly. But now and then we need a genuine treat, a sumptuous celebration of flavors that make the taste buds tingle with ecstasy, like Luscious Louise's Lemon Meringue Pie.

Remember: All things in moderation, including moderation!

ON THE MENU

The Non-Dieter's Delight

Luscious Louise's Lemon Meringue Pie

Larry's Good Eats Grits

Panhead Popcorn With Tasty Toppings

Banana Pecan Cake

Teri's Super Fudge Brownies

Keir's Crunchie Munchies

LUSCIOUS LOUISE'S LEMON MERINGUE PIE

Served with a cup of strong black coffee, a perfect ending to a meal. Be sure to use chocolate wafers for the crust.

SERVES 4

INGREDIENTS

CRUST

21 thin dark, dry chocolate wafers, crushed
⅓ cup melted butter

FILLING

¾ cup (1½ sticks) butter
1½ cups sugar
grated zest of 3 lemons
¼ cup lemon juice
4 eggs plus 1 yolk, beaten

MERINGUE

3 egg whites at room temperature
1 tsp water
⅛ tsp salt
¼ tsp cream of tartar
6 Tbsp powdered sugar
¾ tsp vanilla extract (real—not imitation!)

1. For the crust, mix the crushed wafers and melted butter together well. Press the mixture into a 9-inch pie pan carefully, going up the sides of the pan. Bake in a 350°F oven for about 6 minutes. Cool completely in the pie pan.

2. For the filling, combine and whip the butter, sugar, lemon zest and juice. In a double boiler, cook and stir until melted. Slowly add the beaten eggs and continue cooking until the custard thickens. Cool and pour into the wafer shells.

3. For the meringue, whip the egg whites, water and salt until frothy (about 3 minutes in an electric mixer at high speed). Add the cream of tartar and whip until peaks form, but the mixture is not dry. Add the sugar very slowly by the tablespoon and continue whipping. Make sure all the sugar has dissolved. Fold in the vanilla extract and mix until the meringue stands in peaks.

4. Spread the meringue on top of the filling, forming swirling movements. Bake in a 300°F oven for 20 minutes until browned. Serve at room temperature topped with loads of whipped cream.

THE
NON-DIETER'S DELIGHT
(FRIED BANANAS WITH ICE CREAM)

This is not a dish for dieters – the warm rich sauce and bananas are the perfect mate for the cold ice cream.

SERVES 2 SERIOUS DESSERT EATERS

INGREDIENTS

3 large firm bananas
½ cup (1 stick) butter
¾ cup brown sugar
½ tsp cinnamon
¼ cup banana liqueur
¼ cup rum
super-rich vanilla ice cream

1. Slice the bananas lengthwise and then in half, making four pieces per banana.

2. Use a nonstick skillet to make cleaning it easier. Put the butter in the skillet over low heat. As the butter starts to melt, add the brown sugar and the cinnamon. Stir with a wooden spoon, making sure all the brown sugar has melted.

3. Then add the bananas and cook them for about 3 or 4 minutes, turning the bananas gently so as not to break them. While they are cooking, spoon some of the sauce over them.

4. When the bananas turn light brown, add the banana liqueur and stir for a few minutes. Finally, add the rum and heat for a few more minutes.

5. By this time the sauce should be a rich, brown, bubbling, slightly thick goo. Carefully remove the bananas and divide them between two plates.

6. Turn the heat up under the skillet to thicken the sauce a little more and remove from heat. Put a giant scoop of ice cream on each plate next to the bananas and pour the sauce over both. Serve with a double espresso and the phone number for Weight Watchers.

Variation Put the cooked bananas in a pie dish and pour the sauce over. Put in the refrigerator for about 20 minutes until the sauce slightly hardens. Dish out the bananas and hardened sauce, and serve with ice cream.

"When we were kids and went on family trips in the car, Dad would always pull in at the truck stops for lunch. We would watch out for the place with the most big rigs out front, and that was it.

"It wasn't until I grew up and started traveling on my own that I realized some of the worst food in the country is served in truck stops. Not all of 'em, of course, but the majority are real grease pits. So I figured there were only two reasons for the popularity of truck stops; coffee and parking. But sometimes you'll find a great piece of pie."

Arnold Schwantz, North Dakota

LARRY'S GOOD EATS GRITS

This is a soothing, go-down-easy dessert for a chilly night.

SERVES 2 TO 3

INGREDIENTS

3 cups water
¾ cup grits
6 Tbsp honey
1½ tsp cinnamon
½ cup pecan pieces, chopped not too finely
whipped cream
pecans, to decorate

1. Boil the water; then stir the grits into the pan, lower the heat, and stir until they start to thicken (don't let them boil). Stir in most of the honey and the cinnamon (taste to see if you want more of either). Add the chopped pecans and stir for a few minutes until thick.

2. Pour into two or three soup bowls, top each with a big blob of whipped cream, a sprinkle of cinnamon, and a pecan to decorate.

Note You can also make this with maple syrup or brown sugar instead of the honey if that sounds better.

"The two most perfect foods in the world, without a doubt, are ice cream and chocolate-chip cookies. Only crypto-fascist philistines think otherwise.

"I used to think you could tell something of a person's taste in food by the motorcycle he or she rode. But it ain't so. Of course, you'll see plenty of Harley riders who are certified barbecue junkies, but a batch of 'em are into all kinds of ethnic cuisines. There are more BMW riders eating sushi than there are Asian bike riders into bratwurst. The farther you ride the longer your menu becomes."

Spuds Dooley, Ohio

KEIR'S CRUNCHIE MUNCHIES

Warning: these are addictive. No matter how much you make, they will soon disappear. They can be made with any dry cereals that are not sugar-coated or wimpy like cornflakes or puffed rice. You can also use any combination of spices you like, so feel free to innovate.

MAKES ENOUGH TO FEED AN ARMY OF BIKERS!

INGREDIENTS

2 cups oil
½ cup chili powder
1 Tbsp garlic powder
1 Tbsp onion powder
1 Tbsp paprika
1 Tbsp seafood spice
½ Tbsp cayenne
1 Tbsp liquid smoke
2 or 3 boxes dry cereals, e.g. shredded wheat, corn, rice or bran, about 20 cups in total
2 cups roasted peanuts

1. Put ½ cup of the oil in a saucepan and place over medium heat. When hot, add the spices and "fry" till they sort of dissolve (about 5 minutes). Turn down heat to low and add the remaining oil and the liquid smoke. Stir a few times and cook for another 10 minutes or so.

2. Put the cereals and peanuts into a large baking dish or roasting pan and mix thoroughly. Give the oil mixture a good stir and pour over the cereal mixture. Keep turning the cereal mixture over with a spoon as you pour in the oil to make sure that all the mixture gets coated.

3. Put in a 225°F oven and bake for about 1 hour, turning the mixture over with a spoon every 15 minutes. Serve with ice-cold margaritas.

Note You can eat these warm but they are just as good at room temperature. They keep for weeks when stored in a tightly sealed container.

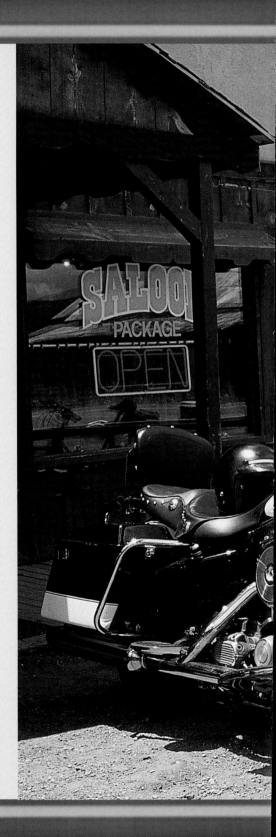

PANHEAD POPCORN WITH TASTY TOPPINGS

Forget that microwaved stuff or the air-popped kind that tastes like cotton wool, this is real popcorn, and for the price of one pack of micro stuff you can pop enough real popcorn to fill your living room.

INGREDIENTS

oil for popping
about ½ cup of unpopped popcorn (you don't need fancy brands)

1. In a large saucepan that has a lid, pour in enough oil to cover the bottom of the pan and heat on medium. Put one kernel of popcorn in the pan until it pops.

2. Pour in the kernels, making sure they are only one layer deep. Turn down the heat to low. The sizzling sound you hear is the moisture escaping. This is important to get crunchy popcorn: when it starts to pop, cover the pan, turn up the heat, and shake, turning up the heat even more until the popping stops. Tip the popcorn into a large bowl.

Variations

• The classic is, of course, melted butter and salt. Or try garlic salt, seasoned salt, onion salt, celery salt, hot paprika, taco spice, or creole spice instead.

• Just after you put the kernels in the pan, add ½ tablespoon of chili powder or curry powder and let simmer along with the unpopped corn.

• Add a tablespoon of sesame oil or macadamia nut oil to the pan when you add the corn.

TERI'S SUPER FUDGE BROWNIES

There are a million recipes for brownies, but these are the fudgiest (and the easiest to make). Decorate or leave plain as they are quite rich.

INGREDIENTS
½ cup (1 stick) butter
4 ounces baking chocolate
2 cups sugar
4 large eggs
1 scant cup all-purpose flour
1 tsp baking powder
dash of salt
1 tsp vanilla extract
optional: ¾ cup pecans or walnuts, not too finely chopped

1. Melt the butter and chocolate together (microwave on low is fine). Mix in the sugar. Mix in the eggs *one at a time*. Mix in the flour and baking powder, then the salt, vanilla and the nuts (if you are a brownies with nuts person). All this can be done in one bowl and mixed by hand.

2. Pour into a greased 13- × 9-inch baking pan. Bake on the middle shelf of a 350°F oven for about 25-35 minutes. The secret is not to overcook them so that they stay moist and fudgie. Check doneness with a toothpick after 25 minutes. If lots of batter sticks to the toothpick, bake for another 5 minutes and test again. If still not done, try 5 more. Since ovens vary, it is hard to be more precise but once you get it right, you can enjoy these forever. Remove from the oven and let cool. Cut into 20 pieces.

Note These taste best while still warm and served with an ice-cold glass of milk or a big scoop of super-rich vanilla ice cream. If there are any left, they do keep tightly wrapped in plastic wrap.

"You wouldn't think that riding a motorcycle would help you work up a big appetite. But you can use up a good number of calories on the open road, and it's best to replenish them.

"I suppose it depends on your metabolism; I've seen skinny folks who don't eat much of anything very often, and they seem to get along fine. But I know that I go groggy if I spend too much time in the saddle without eating. I always eat a little something whenever I stop for gas. It's good to stretch the legs and refuel the stomach."

Glen Morton, Virginia

BANANA PECAN CAKE

A delicious combo of bananas and pecans topped with a rich maple frosting. It only needs a cup of strong black coffee as an accompaniment.

INGREDIENTS

3 large ripe bananas
½ cup (1 stick) butter
1½ cups sugar
2 large eggs
½ tsp baking soda
½ cup buttermilk
2 cups all-purpose flour, sifted
½ tsp baking powder
½ cup chopped pecans
¼ cup pecan halves, to decorate

FROSTING

3 cups powdered sugar
2 Tbsp butter, softened
5 Tbsp maple syrup
3 Tbsp heavy cream
pinch of salt

1. Mash the bananas and mix in the butter and sugar. Beat in the eggs one at a time. Dissolve the baking soda in the buttermilk and mix in. Add the flour, baking powder, and pecans and mix well.

2. Pour into two 9-inch buttered layer cake pans . Bake in a 350°F for about 30-35 minutes until done. Test with a toothpick to determine if done. Cool in the pans for 10 minutes, then turn onto a wire rack to cool completely.

3. To make the frosting, sift the sugar into a bowl and make a well in the center. Add the butter, maple syrup, cream, and salt, gradually incorporating into the sugar. Beat well until smooth. Working quickly, spread one-third of the frosting over one cake and place the other cake on top. Spread the remaining frosting over the top and sides of the whole cake. Decorate with pecan halves.

Note The frosting sets quickly.

ACKNOWLEDGMENTS

No book is a totally individual effort, and this one is no exception. I wish to thank: two great New Orleans cooks, Louise Washington and Melanie Feldman, my 'fax mates', who were a constant source of information and help; Jane Donovan (Project Manager), Kathryn Hawkins (Home Economist and Food Stylist), Jon Stewart (Photographer) and Roger Hyde (Designer), who all contributed to the great look of the book, and the tempting pictures of the recipes; Keir and Sarah Helberg were also a great help, not least for allowing me to make use of their extensive library; my cousin Teri Dobrow, for acting as the keeper and custodian of my mother's recipes; and Philip de Ste. Croix, who developed the idea for this book in the first place. And a special acknowledgment must go to Nancy Davis of Random House Value Publishing, without whose ideas this book would not have been the way it is.

Special thanks to Gerry Mars, my fax man, my son Benjamin for being a guinea pig and, last but certainly not least, to dearest Sara: taster, washer-upper, cutter-upper, shopper and moral supporter.

INDEX

Appetizers 21
Au Gratin, Crab &
    Shrimp 44

Banana Pecan Cake 75
Bananas, Fried with Ice Cream 71
Bean, Mean Green, Casserole 54
Beans, Good Old Boys'
    Barbecued 50
BBQ
    Chicken Wings, Sweet Jean's 39
    Marinade, Carolina 67
    Short Ribs, Lenny's Lemon 31
    Shrimp, Bubba's Original 46
Beef Barbecue, Ricki
    Sue's 34
Beef Tacos, Bad
    Boy 32
Biscuits, American
    Heritage 18
Breakfast 15
Brisket, Marty's
    Brewhouse 35
Brownies, Teri's Super Fudge 74
Brunch 15
Buffalo Wings, Billy's 25

Cake, Banana Pecan 75
Casserole, Mean Green Bean 54
Chicken, Blue Bayou
    Fried 40
Chicken, Sara Liz's
    Garlic & Honey 38
Chicken Wings, Sweet
    Jean's BBQ 39
Chili, Louise Washington's
    Best 33
Chops, Fat Sam's Stuffed
    Pork 32
Cooking Hints 11
Corn Bread, Kickstart 18
Crab & Shrimp Au
    Gratin 44
Desserts 69
Dressing,
    Dutch's Mustard Mayo 66
    Guido's Creamy Garlic 66
    Nutty Parmesan 65
    Rudy's Russian 65
Dressings 63

Dunking Sauce, Sweet-Funky 67

Fish 43
Bike Club Soda Fried 47
French Toast, Cheesy 16

Garlic Dressing, Guido's Creamy, 66
Gravy, Red Eye 29
Grits,
    Jalapeño Horsepower, 19
    Larry's Good Eats, 72
Guacamole 28
Gyros, Pit Stop 61

Hamburgers, Spread It On 59
Ham Steak, Fried,
    & Red Eye Gravy 29
Hot Dogs, Da Bears' 59

Ice Cream, Fried Bananas with 71

Lasagne, Nicole's Nostalgia 34
Lemon Meringue Pie, Luscious
    Louise's 70

Macaroni & Cheese, Mark's 51
Marinades 63
Mashed Potatoes,
    Dial 911, 53
Matzos, Cajun Fried 18
Meatball Sub, Mario's 61
Meat Dishes 27
Meatloaf, Torque Master 30
Mozzarella Sticks, Manny's
    Fried 24
Munchies, Keir's Crunchie 72
Mushrooms, Thunder Grunt
    Stuffed 22
Mustard Mayo Dressing, Dutch's 66

Nachos, Norm's Nasty 23
Non-Dieter's Delight, The 71

Okra, Robyn's Spicy Fried 53
Omelet, El Paso 17

Pancakes, Suzie's
    Sour Cream 16
Parmesan, Nutty, Dressing 65
Pit Stop Gyros 61
Pie, Luscious Louise's
    Lemon Meringue 70
Po' Boy, Rich Man's 60
Popcorn, Panhead with Tasty
    Toppings 73

Pork Chops, Fat Sam's
    Stuffed 32
Potato Salad, Dave's
    Deluxe 52
Potato, Spuds Rodriguez' Hot 55
Potatoes, Dial 911, Mashed 53
Poultry 37

Rich Man's Po' Boy 60
Russian Dressing, Rudy's 65

Salad, Dave's Deluxe
    Potato 52
Salads 49
Sandwich, The Don's Sausage
    & Pepper 58
Sandwiches 57
Sauce, Frenchy LeBec's Steak 64
Sauce, Mi Hung's Mustard 66
Sauce, Sweet-Funky Dunking 67
Sauces 63
Sausage & Pepper Sandwich,
    The Don's 58
Seafood 43
Seafood Salad, Sal
    Calamari's 45
Shortcuts 11—12
Short Ribs, Lenny's
    Lemon BBQ 31
Shrimp,
    (& Crab), Au Gratin 44
    Bubba's Original BBQ 46
Skirt Steak, Carmelita's Fajita,
    with Guacamole, 28
Snacks 69
Soup, Claude's Blue
    Cheese 24
Spareribs,
    Benjie's Beijing 30
    Lone Star BBQ 28
Steak,
    Ham, Fried (& Red Eye Gravy) 29
    Sauce, Frenchy LeBec's 64

Tacos, Bad Boy
    Beef 32
Toast, French 16
Turkey, Down Home
    Deep-fried 41

Vegetables 49

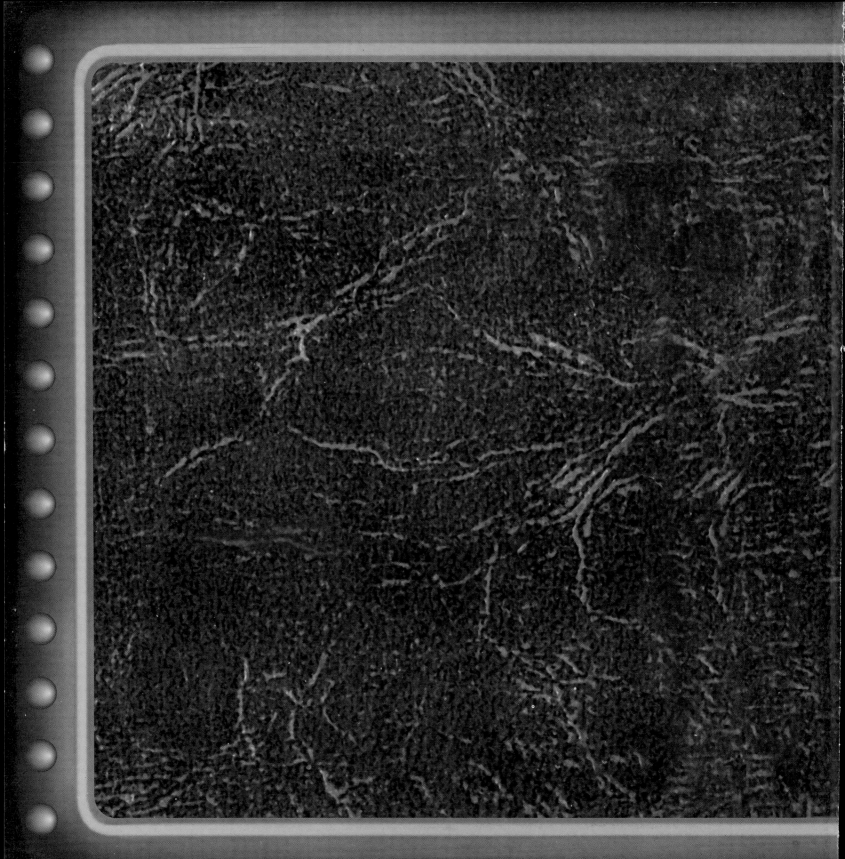